# Marketing Strategies for Changing Times

Wellford W. Wilms, *Editor*
*University of California, Los Angeles*

Richard W. Moore, *Editor*
*Training Research Corporation*

---

**NEW DIRECTIONS FOR COMMUNITY COLLEGES**
ARTHUR M. COHEN, *Editor-in-Chief*
FLORENCE B. BRAWER, *Associate Editor*

Number 60, Winter 1987

Paperback sourcebooks in
The Jossey-Bass Higher Education Series

Jossey-Bass Inc., Publishers
San Francisco • London

EDUCATIONAL RESOURCES INFORMATION CENTER

**Clearinghouse For Junior Colleges**

UNIVERSITY OF CALIFORNIA, LOS ANGELES

Wellford W. Wilms, Richard W. Moore (eds.).
*Marketing Strategies for Changing Times.*
New Directions for Community Colleges, no. 60.
Volume XV, number 4.
San Francisco: Jossey-Bass, 1987.

*New Directions for Community Colleges*
Arthur M. Cohen, *Editor-in-Chief;* Florence B. Brawer, *Associate Editor*

*New Directions for Community Colleges* is published quarterly by Jossey-Bass
Inc., Publishers (publication number USPS 121-710), in association with the
ERIC Clearinghouse for Junior Colleges. *New Directions* is numbered
sequentially—please order extra copies by sequential number. The volume and
issue numbers above are included for the convenience of libraries. Second-class
postage paid at San Francisco, California, and at additional mailing offices.
POSTMASTER: Send address changes to Jossey-Bass, Inc., Publishers,
433 California Street, San Francisco, California 94104.

The material in this publication was prepared pursuant to a contract with
the Office of Educational Research and Improvement, U.S. Department of
Education. Contractors undertaking such projects under government
sponsorship are encouraged to express freely their judgment in professional and
technical matters. Prior to publication, the manuscript was submitted to the
Center for the Study of Community Colleges for critical review and
determination of professional competence. This publication has met such
standards. Points of view or opinions, however, do not necessarily represent the
official view or opinions of the Center for the Study of Community Colleges or
the Office of Educational Research and Improvement.

**Editorial correspondence** should be sent to the Editor-in-Chief, Arthur M.
Cohen, at the ERIC Clearinghouse for Junior Colleges, University of
California, Los Angeles, California 90024.

Library of Congress Catalog Card Number LC 85-644753

International Standard Serial Number ISSN 0194-3081

International Standard Book Number ISBN 1-55542-952-1

Cover art by WILLI BAUM

Manufactured in the United States of America

# Ordering Information

The paperback sourcebooks listed below are published quarterly and can be ordered either by subscription or single copy.

Subscriptions cost $52.00 per year for institutions, agencies, and libraries. Individuals can subscribe at the special rate of $39.00 per year *if payment is by personal check.* (Note that the full rate of $52.00 applies if payment is by institutional check, even if the subscription is designated for an individual.) Standing orders are accepted.

Single copies are available at $12.95 when payment accompanies order. (California, New Jersey, New York, and Washington, D.C., residents please include appropriate sales tax.) For billed orders, cost per copy is $12.95 plus postage and handling.

Substantial discounts are offered to organizations and individuals wishing to purchase bulk quantities of Jossey-Bass sourcebooks. Please inquire.

Please note that these prices are for the academic year 1987–88 and are subject to change without notice. Also, some titles may be out of print and therefore not available for sale.

To ensure correct and prompt delivery, all orders must give either the *name of an individual* or an *official purchase order number.* Please submit your order as follows:

*Subscriptions:* specify series and year subscription is to begin.
*Single Copies:* specify sourcebook code (such as, CC1) and first two words of title.

Mail orders for United States and Possessions, Australia, New Zealand, Canada, Latin America, and Japan to:
Jossey-Bass Inc., Publishers
433 California Street
San Francisco, California 94104

Mail orders for all other parts of the world to:
Jossey-Bass Limited
28 Banner Street
London EC1Y 8QE

*New Directions for Community Colleges Series*
Arthur M. Cohen, *Editor-in-Chief*
Florence B. Brawer, *Associate Editor*

CC1    *Toward a Professional Faculty,* Arthur M. Cohen
CC2    *Meeting the Financial Crisis,* John Lombardi
CC3    *Understanding Diverse Students,* Dorothy M. Knoell

CC4  *Updating Occupational Education,* Norman C. Harris
CC5  *Implementing Innovative Instruction,* Roger H. Garrison
CC6  *Coordinating State Systems,* Edmund J. Gleazer, Jr., Roger Yarrington
CC7  *From Class to Mass Learning,* William M. Birenbaum
CC8  *Humanizing Student Services,* Clyde E. Blocker
CC9  *Using Instructional Technology,* George H. Voegel
CC10 *Reforming College Governance,* Richard C. Richardson, Jr.
CC11 *Adjusting to Collective Bargaining,* Richard J. Ernst
CC12 *Merging the Humanities,* Leslie Koltai
CC13 *Changing Managerial Perspectives,* Barry Heermann
CC14 *Reaching Out Through Community Service,* Hope M. Holcomb
CC15 *Enhancing Trustee Effectiveness,* Victoria Dziuba, William Meardy
CC16 *Easing the Transition from Schooling to Work,* Harry F. Silberman,
      Mark B. Ginsburg
CC17 *Changing Instructional Strategies,* James O. Hammons
CC18 *Assessing Student Academic and Social Progress,* Leonard L. Baird
CC19 *Developing Staff Potential,* Terry O'Banion
CC20 *Improving Relations with the Public,* Louis W. Bender,
      Benjamin R. Wygal
CC21 *Implementing Community-Based Education,* Ervin L. Harlacher,
      James F. Gollattscheck
CC22 *Coping with Reduced Resources,* Richard L. Alfred
CC23 *Balancing State and Local Control,* Searle F. Charles
CC24 *Responding to New Missions,* Myron A. Marty
CC25 *Shaping the Curriculum,* Arthur M. Cohen
CC26 *Advancing International Education,* Maxwell C. King, Robert L. Breuder
CC27 *Serving New Populations,* Patricia Ann Walsh
CC28 *Managing in a New Era,* Robert E. Lahti
CC29 *Serving Lifelong Learners,* Barry Heermann, Cheryl Coppeck Enders,
      Elizabeth Wine
CC30 *Using Part-Time Faculty Effectively,* Michael H. Parsons
CC31 *Teaching the Sciences,* Florence B. Brawer
CC32 *Questioning the Community College Role,* George B. Vaughan
CC33 *Occupational Education Today,* Kathleen F. Arns
CC34 *Women in Community Colleges,* Judith S. Eaton
CC35 *Improving Decision Making,* Mantha Mehallis
CC36 *Marketing the Program,* William A. Keim, Marybelle C. Keim
CC37 *Organization Development: Change Strategies,* James Hammons
CC38 *Institutional Impacts on Campus, Community, and Business Constituencies,*
      Richard L. Alfred
CC39 *Improving Articulation and Transfer Relationships,* Frederick C. Kintzer
CC40 *General Education in Two-Year Colleges,* B. Lamar Johnson
CC41 *Evaluating Faculty and Staff,* Al Smith
CC42 *Advancing the Liberal Arts,* Stanley F. Turesky
CC43 *Counseling: A Crucial Function for the 1980s,* Alice S. Thurston,
      William A. Robbins
CC44 *Strategic Management in the Community College,* Gunder A. Myran
CC45 *Designing Programs for Community Groups,* S. V. Martorana,
      William E. Piland
CC46 *Emerging Roles for Community College Leaders,* Richard L. Alfred,
      Paul A. Elsner, R. Jan LeCroy, Nancy Armes
CC47 *Microcomputer Applications in Administration and Instruction,*
      Donald A. Dellow, Lawrence H. Poole

CC48   *Customized Job Training for Business and Industry*, Robert J. Kopecek, Robert G. Clarke

CC49   *Ensuring Effective Governance*, William L. Deegan, James F. Gollattscheck

CC50   *Strengthening Financial Management*, Dale F. Campbell

CC51   *Active Trusteeship for a Changing Era*, Gary Frank Petty

CC52   *Maintaining Institutional Integrity*, Donald E. Puyear, George B. Vaughan

CC53   *Controversies and Decision Making in Difficult Economic Times*, Billie Wright Dziech

CC54   *The Community College and Its Critics*, L. Stephen Zwerling

CC55   *Advances in Instructional Technology*, George H. Voegel

CC56   *Applying Institutional Research*, John Losak

CC57   *Teaching the Developmental Education Student*, Kenneth M. Ahrendt

CC58   *Developing Occupational Programs*, Charles R. Doty

CC59   *Issues in Student Assessment*, Dorothy Bray, Marcia J. Belcher

# Contents

*Editors' Notes*                                                        1
*Wellford W. Wilms, Richard W. Moore*

**1. Marching to the Market: A New Tune for Training**                   5
**Organizations**
*Wellford W. Wilms*
Only by staying closely attuned to their student and employer markets
can community colleges and proprietary institutions hope to weather the
storms of a changing future.

**2. California's Employment Training Panel: Creating Incentives**       15
**for Change**
*Steve Duscha*
In California, the Employment Training Panel provides a model of
schools working cooperatively with business and workers to meet the
demands of the economic marketplace.

**3. Performance Contracting: Successfully Managing the Risk**           23
*Linda M. Thor*
Performance contracting places a community college's ability to recover
its investment in employment training at risk, and whether the college
breaks even, makes a profit, or loses money depends on its ability to manage the risk.

**4. Maintaining Links with Local Employers: The Key to**               33
**Proprietary School Success**
*Dean Johnston*
Close ties with employers, appropriate programs, a dedicated faculty and
staff, and a qualified and committed placement director are essential to
the success of all career-training institutions.

**5. Increasing Enrollments: A Marketing Perspective**                  41
*Michael K. Brannick*
Imposing the marketing concept on all aspects of school and college oper-
ations can pay off in increased enrollments.

**6. A 1980s Approach to Planning: The Houston Community**              51
**College System**
*Joyce Boatright, Jacquelin Crowley*
The Houston Community College System used marketing research in the
development of professional training seminars for the adult business
community.

*7. Student Recruitment: A Market Research Primer*                61
*Richard W. Moore*

Market research techniques provide educators with tools that allow them to systematically follow the changing student market and respond promptly to emerging trends.

*8. Public Relations and Marketing*                75
*Daniel D. Savage*

Proactive public relations involves a deliberate effort to project an image of the college that can change public attitudes and win community support.

*9. Summary and Conclusions*                83
*Wellford W. Wilms, Richard W. Moore*

The editors summarize highlights of the individual chapters and draw conclusions about how institutions can succeed in a rapidly changing environment.

*10. Sources and Information: Reaching Employer and*                87
*Student Markets*
*Anita Y. Colby, Mary P. Hardy*

Further information on succeeding in a changing market is provided by the ERIC Clearinghouse for Junior Colleges.

*Index*                105

# Editors' Notes

Community colleges and proprietary vocational schools (privately owned postsecondary schools that operate for profit) are directly connected to their communities. Both types of institutions depend on attracting local students and placing them in jobs with local employers. Thus, community colleges' and proprietary schools' links with students and employers are of paramount importance. However, the communities served by these colleges and schools are being reshaped by forces that are far removed from the immediate concerns of administrators. Changing demographics, new technologies, an increasingly competitive international economy, and declining resources for education are factors that administrators must now consider if they are to effectively navigate in this uncertain future. As educational resources have shrunk, policy makers have begun to demand that institutions become more productive and efficient. Such demands have taken the form of *performance contracting* for job training, meaning that if trainees fail to get jobs, training agencies are not paid. Thus, performance contracting for training under the federal Job Training Partnership Act and California's Employment Training Panel has become of major interest to colleges and schools.

The theme of this volume is "Succeeding in a Changing Market." In our view, successful administrators must be able to appeal to two distinct and rapidly changing markets: students and employers. The opening chapter, by Wellford W. Wilms, provides an overview of the shifting world economy and examines the forces that are reshaping both student and employer markets. Wilms questions whether public institutions' incentives, which have been purposely designed to provide them with stability, will allow them to adapt successfully to a rapidly changing environment. In the remainder of the volume, authors who are practitioners and researchers discuss ways in which community colleges and proprietary schools have been able to cope with changes in the employer and student markets.

## Employer Markets

The first half of this volume explores different aspects of employer markets. Chapter Two, by Steve Duscha, questions the wisdom of spending public funds for job training unless jobs can be assured for trainees. He shows how performance contracting ensures that public monies are well spent by guaranteeing that training leads directly to employment. Duscha also emphasizes the importance of job training as a tool for economic development.

1

Chapter Three, by Linda M. Thor, examines another aspect of performance contracting—managing risk that is inherent in such contracts. Thor compares results of training, under both the federal Job Training Partnership Act and California's Employment Training Panel, from the perspective of the college administrator. She details strategies that colleges have used to manage risk under performance contracting.

Another way of managing risk in a changing environment is to firmly link the school or college with local employers, so that shifting demand for employees can be quickly translated into new programs. In Chapter Four, Dean Johnston examines how a small proprietary college, rooted in a community, can develop employer networks to place students in jobs while tracking market changes.

## Student Markets

The second half of this volume provides concrete steps administrators may take to effectively market their programs. It includes an annotated bibliography (Chapter Ten) by Anita Y. Colby and Mary P. Hardy.

In Chapter Five, Michael K. Brannick describes how market research concepts can be applied to job training and education. Brannick takes readers step-by-step through ways his firm analyzes its markets and does strategic planning.

In Chapter Six, Joyce Boatright and Jacquelin Crowley describe how the Houston Community College District used marketing concepts to increase its enrollments and its service to the local business community.

In Chapter Seven, Richard W. Moore discusses how schools have used such specific market research techniques as focus groups, demographic studies, and consumer surveys to track student market trends. Moore's chapter also includes an annotated bibliography of selected references on market research in education.

In Chapter Eight, Daniel D. Savage shows the value of public relations communicating with the larger public about changes in a college's local market. Savage also provides practical advice about how to set up and organize a public relations office in a community college.

## Conclusion

In Chapter Nine, the editors summarize highlights of the individual chapters and draw conclusions about how institutions can successfully cope with a rapidly changing environment.

Wellford W. Wilms
Richard W. Moore
Editors

*Wellford W. Wilms is associate professor and assistant dean of
students in the Graduate School of Education at the
University of California, Los Angeles.*

*Richard W. Moore is the executive director of Training
Research Corporation.*

*Community colleges and proprietary institutions must stay closely attuned to their markets.*

# Marching to the Market: A New Tune for Training Organizations

*Wellford W. Wilms*

Anyone who thinks that the world is changing had better look again—it has already changed. As Drucker (1986) notes, the United States has moved from a national to a world economy, in which the primary products economy (petroleum and steel, for example) has become uncoupled from the traditional industrial economy because of new production processes and new products. In turn, the industrial economy has become uncoupled from employment, and the movement of capital (rather than trade) has become the driving force.

Over the past few years, the center of the world economy has dramatically shifted, from Western Europe and the eastern United States to the Pacific Rim nations. Twenty-five years ago, who would have thought that today England would be on the economic scrap heap? Three years ago, who would have thought that Korea would be manufacturing automobiles for sale in the United States and would boast the most advanced steel production in the world? As recently as a year ago, who would have thought that the People's Republic of China would be exporting food?

Because of these rapid changes in the world economy, even Japan must scramble to compete with the "Little Dragons" (Singapore, Hong

W. W. Wilms and R. W. Moore (eds.). *Marketing Strategies for Changing Times.*
New Directions for Community Colleges, no. 60. San Francisco: Jossey-Bass, Winter 1987.

Kong, and Taiwan), which are investing heavily in their own assembly plants and in the infrastructure necessary for world competition. The impact of these shifts on U.S. foreign trade has been severe. It is estimated that for every $1 billion lost in trade, 25,000 jobs are lost as well.

Not surprisingly, then, productivity has become a new national preoccupation. Private firms, government agencies, and educational institutions are urged to be more productive. Because of their direct link to the labor market, community colleges and proprietary vocational schools, in particular, are asked to do more with less in an increasingly competitive and unpredictable world.

## Harbingers of Change

If they are to be successful in planning programs that will meet contemporary demands and in attracting students who can benefit from these programs, school and college administrators must be aware of these rapid shifts in the economy, especially of changes in student demographics and technology.

Nationally, changing demographics affect both the supply and the demand for job training and education. Most observers agree that the labor force will grow steadily, from 110 million workers today to about 131 million in 1995. Women, who now constitute 39 percent of the labor force, are expected to account for 47 percent in 1995. The proportion of black workers is predicted to increase from 10 percent to 15 percent, whereas the proportion of young adults (between sixteen and twenty-four years of age) will drop from 22 percent to 8 percent (U.S. Bureau of the Census, 1986). Obviously, student demographics will vary considerably from one region to another, but few community colleges or proprietary schools can continue to bank on enrolling large numbers of white eighteen-year-olds—the mainstay of their student bodies for the past two decades. Instead, most institutions have begun to analyze alternative markets (for example, older students, minority students) and to seek ways of adjusting their programs to accommodate these students' needs.

Because of the press for productivity, employers, too, have changed the way they do business. A growing number of U.S. firms are investing in technology to boost productivity and to improve their competitiveness in the world economy. Despite widespread agreement that new technologies affect the demand for education, opinions differ on just what those effects are. One view holds that technology raises skill requirements in upper-level jobs but reduces them in lower-level jobs. For example, a study of New York City employers found no evidence that new technology creates more jobs requiring advanced skills (Lynton, 1979). Indeed, the number of lower-level jobs had increased in some of the industries studied, widening the gap between skilled and unskilled workers.

Similarly, more than two-thirds of a sample of Los Angeles area employers reported that improved technology had produced no change in skill requirements (Wilms, 1984). The lower the job level, the smaller the impact of technology. Thus, while changing technology had had almost no effect on unskilled jobs and only a slight effect on clerical jobs, it had led to increased skill requirements for about one-third of professional, technical, managerial, and sales jobs. In support of this view, Levin and Rumberger (1983) observe that while more and more jobs are affected by technology, most new equipment is very easy to operate, and new skills can be learned on the job.

Likewise, some experts expect that robots will dramatically reshape work on the shop floor, and will thus affect education and training requirements, but as Levitan (1984) points out, this impact will probably be limited, at least for the foreseeable future, because robots cost so much. For example, General Electric was reported to have spent $316 million in refitting a conventional locomotive plant with state-of-the-art technology. Clearly, only the largest and healthiest U.S. firms can afford such expensive technology. Further, in their study of manufacturing practices, Krafcik and Womack (1987) concluded that gains in productivity derive not so much from technology alone as from its integration into a plant's social structure. In any event, most observers think that work itself is not going to change very radically, despite the introduction of new technologies.

In contrast, the occupational structure is expected to undergo substantial change, with nearly half the projected growth concentrated in forty job classifications, most of which pay relatively little and require little education or training. The ten job classifications expected to contribute the largest number of jobs are building custodian, cashier, secretary, clerk, nurse, waiter, teacher, truck driver, nursing aide/orderly, and sales representative. In contrast, most of the jobs in the fastest-growing occupations (including computer service technician, legal assistant, computer systems analyst, and programmer) pay relatively well and require more education and training (U.S. Bureau of Labor Statistics, 1986) but, because of their small base, contribute far fewer jobs to the overall economy.

Noting the disproportionate growth in low-level, low-paying jobs, some observers characterize tomorrow's labor market as lacking a middle, and they fear that it may polarize society into haves and have-nots. There are some data to support this hypothesis. For example, according to Bluestone (1983), between 1960 and 1975 the highest- and lowest-earning classes increased as proportions of the total labor force, whereas the proportion in the middle of the job distribution declined. Rumberger and Levin (1984) believe that the number of low-skilled jobs will expand much faster than the number of high-skilled jobs. Thus, the demand for computer programmers is expected to reach 150,000 by 1990, whereas the demand for janitors is projected to be nearly nine times as large, reaching 1.3 million in the same year.

Evidence of sustained growth in the service sector—growth largely attributable to shifts in demography and in student tastes—also supports the hypothesis of a polarized labor force. Moreover, as two-income families become more common, demand for such services as real estate sales, insurance, housecleaning, daycare, and education will increase, and as the population ages, increased health care services will be required.

Whatever the shape of the future job market, most observers agree that major changes are occurring, and with increasing speed. The question of how to adapt school and college programs to these unpredictable shifts has thus become a central concern for educators.

**Barriers to Change**

In attempting to make these adaptations, educators face some formidable barriers. Chief among them are the current methods of financing education, especially public education. Community colleges are financed in large part through formulas that allocate funds on the basis of each institution's average daily attendance. Thus, community colleges are motivated to enroll as many students as possible, without much regard for outcomes.

Public institutions also receive substantial funding through federal job training legislation, the Job Training Partnership Act and the Perkins Vocational Education Act in particular. Until recently, however, funding under these programs and their predecessors was based largely on supply-side considerations, without much regard for demand. Between World War II and the 1960s, an expanding economy and ample resources for training obviated the need for much planning. Then, beginning in the 1960s, the civil rights movement inspired various constituent groups (blacks, Hispanics, Native Americans, women, lesbians and gays, the disabled, and, more recently, displaced workers) to demand a share of training resources. In response to these demands, job training legislation provides that resources be distributed according to fixed formulas. For example, the Perkins Vocational Education Act requires that funds be allocated as follows: 10 percent for disabled students; 22 percent for students from disadvantaged backgrounds, with 3 percent going to students who speak only limited English; 12 percent for adults who need job training; 8.5 percent for single parents; and so forth. Thus, constituents' demands have become embedded in each piece of significant legislation, limiting institutional ability to adapt to rapidly changing external demands.

Another limitation on institutional flexibility is American tradition, which gives high priority to consumer demand for education and training. According to this tradition, those who attend public institutions have the right to select the fields in which they want to be educated, independent of whether or not a demand exists. In the words of Bolton (1985), former head of California's Assembly Office of Research: "If 2,000 young people come to a community college to be trained as secretaries and the funding is available to train them, then you'll train them because they are taxpayers and they have the right to demand what they want."

Finally, current methods of allocating funds for training are not efficient in targeting them to where they are most needed and will do the most good. For example, Title III of the Job Training Partnership Act stipulates that 70 percent of all funds be spent on the retraining of displaced workers, a substantial amount of which is done by community colleges and proprietary vocational schools. As more and more studies indicate, however, only about one in five of the workers displaced by plant closures opts for training. According to a study of twenty-two California reemployment projects, only 19 percent of the nearly 20,000 persons eligible to participate actually enrolled in retraining programs. The majority needed income immediately, because of family obligations, and simply could not afford to take the time required. Moreover, many displaced workers lacked the basic reading, writing, and computational abilities that are frequently prerequisites for formal training (California Employment Development Department, 1983). In short, these factors—the allocation of funds through average-daily-attendance formulas, the practice of reserving training funds for powerful constituent groups, and the American tradition of giving consumer choice a high priority even though it may have little to do with market demand—all operate to keep public training institutions detached from changing labor market conditions. Obviously, incentives are needed to strengthen the link.

### Performance Contracting: Cash on Delivery

In response to growing demands for improved economic productivity, new policies are emerging. One significant aspect of these new policies is the emphasis on linking job training to market demand by paying training institutions only after trainees have been successful in finding jobs. This approach, called *performance training,* is modeled after educational experiments tried first in the early part of the nineteenth century in Georgia and later in Ontario, Canada. Under these performance contracts, schools were paid on the basis of how well their students performed on standardized tests. According to research on the effects of performance contracting in these educational settings, students' test scores could be quickly raised if subject matter was narrowly defined and students were intensively trained ("The Customers Pass the Test—or Else," 1970). The evidence further indicated that teachers, anxious to be paid, concentrated their efforts on the more able students, to the exclusion of others. Not surprisingly, the public voiced opposition to the sacrifice of broad educational values for narrow ends, and the approach was abandoned. Educational performance contracting was tried again under the Nixon administration. In 1969–1970, 170 school districts contracted with private firms to teach reading and math to high school dropouts. Whatever enthusiasm the public may have had for the plan quickly waned, however, when federal audits showed that students were being taught specific answers to test questions.

Thus, experience with performance contracting suggests that it may be inappropriate to educational settings. Tying payments to test performance drives institutions to restrict subject matter to narrow topics, to favor those students who are likely to succeed, and simply to drill them on these narrow topics.

Although performance contracting may be inappropriate to educational purposes, it is better suited to the more straightforward and measureable task of job training. Further, its built-in incentives for selecting trainees who are likely to succeed can only help when it comes to targeting job training funds more efficiently and, ultimately, to improving industrial as well as educational productivity. The growing interest in improving productivity by orienting training institutions to market demand is reflected in the central role given to performance contracting in both the federal Job Training Partnership Act (see Chapter Two) and in California's Employment Training Panel (see Chapter Three).

Under performance contracts, trainers are not paid until trainees have successfully completed training and are placed in private-sector jobs. Consequently, community college and proprietary school administrators have powerful economic incentives to make sure that their programs are closely linked to the shifting demands of students and of the labor market.

**Institutional Incentives in a Changing Environment**

While performance contracting dramatically changes the environment in which some community colleges and proprietary schools operate, institutions that do not enter into such contracts must find other ways of adjusting their programs to the changing environment. To what extent can institutional administrators successfully alter the course of their institutions?

The institutional incentives that drive community colleges differ radically from those that drive proprietary vocational schools. An analysis of these differences gives some clues to how the two types of institutions are likely to behave in an environment marked by rapid and unpredictable fluctuations in supply and demand, stemming from worldwide economic adjustments.

In concept, community colleges and proprietary schools differ primarily in their relationships to markets. Proprietary schools are best described as market-oriented organizations, whose income depends on whether customers buy their products or services. Such organizations tend to have relatively simple goals and objectives. Because they base their personnel decisions as well as their resource allocations on market demands, managers must consider signals from output markets if the organizations are to survive and operate profitably (Wilms, 1974).

The proprietary school industry is heterogeneous, with schools that offer instruction in diverse subjects, from accounting to zookeeping. While their variety may seem endless, they fall into four main categories: cosmetology and barber schools, trade (including aviation, industrial arts, and allied health) schools, business and secretarial institutions, and a handful of correspondence schools and others that cannot be easily categorized.

The proprietary school industry is also the largest school-based purveyor of vocational training (Wilms, 1987). Because they are businesses first and educational institutions second, proprietary schools are aggressive in their marketing, advertising, and cost-management techniques. They derive their income solely from student tuitions, and so they must hold out the promise of successful job placement to attract students. Consequently, as Johnston (Chapter Four) and Brannick (Chapter Five) point out, successful school owners must pay attention not only to student markets but also to signals from employers.

Proprietary school teachers are usually recruited from business and industry. Generally, they are hired for their teaching ability; formal educational credentials count for little. Faculty members are not unionized, nor do they receive tenure. They are evaluated frequently, and promotions and pay raises are based heavily on these evaluations (Wilms, 1984).

The typical proprietary school offers only two or three vocational programs, adding or dropping one program every two years. School owners report that their decisions to add new programs are most frequently prompted by direct employer requests, whereas declining enrollments and difficult job placements are chief reasons for dropping programs (Wilms, 1984).

In contrast, many public organizations in capitalistic democracies carry out social functions that cannot be entrusted solely to private interests: regulating air travel (the Civil Aeronautics Board), collecting taxes (the Internal Revenue Service), and providing services that have indivisible benefits (public schools) (Downs, 1967). These organizations tend to be large. They depend on full-time staffs, and they base their personnel decisions on merit, with little regard for output markets.

While they must compete with other nonmarket organizations for resources, their products are not directly evaluated in output markets. Thus, their income, and hence their survival, depend not on the marketplace but on their ability to deal with the political process that ultimately governs them. For example, community colleges depend on federal, state, and local political processes for their income and survival and are thus subject to varied and often conflicting signals about their mission and priorities. On the one hand, they provide the first two years of college work to students planning to transfer to four-year institutions; on the other, they offer vocational training to another student clientele. Faculty members are appointed largely on the basis of academic degrees and previous teaching experience. Employment security is protected through a tenure system, and community college faculties are typically unionized.

Lacking direct connections to output markets, nonmarket-oriented organizations must use other devices to guide resource allocation. Probably the most common of these devices is last year's budget, of primary importance in determining this year's budget, because it represents agreement. Ensuring that community colleges, like most other public institutions, are not directly dependent on output markets for their survival also ensures their stability over time. Budget and program changes are usually small and incremental. Most important, they may be unrelated to new market needs. Once established, vocational programs tend to perpetuate themselves and are slow to adjust to new conditions (California Commission on Industrial Innovations, 1982; Grubb and Jassaud, 1984).

**Meeting the Challenge**

There is little doubt that community colleges and proprietary schools alike will be affected by demands for the increased productivity that will enable the United States to compete more effectively in the world economy. Further, simply by counting noses, one can see that far fewer young whites and many more women, blacks, and Hispanics will enroll in these institutions on their way to employment in the near future. Thus, purveyors of vocational education must adapt their programs to appeal to these nontraditional students and to answer the needs of a rapidly changing labor market.

Clearly, performance contracting represents a significant trend. By tying payment to performance, this policy requires that community colleges and proprietary schools pay close attention to changing events. Nevertheless, it is probably only one of many steps that successful institutions have already taken to stay ahead of the curve. As we have seen, proprietary schools' dependence for survival on student tuitions keeps them closely attuned to market shifts. Moreover, plunging enrollments at many community colleges have forced them to jump many of the barriers that keep them insulated from markets and to adopt aggressive marketing and advertising strategies. For instance, some of them have hired special-ized marketing consultants to help them better position themselves in the shrinking student market and to differentiate their programs from those of their competitors.

Many college presidents who would have turned up their noses a decade ago at the idea of advertising for students are now turning to the mass media in order to survive. When Leslie Koltai, chancellor of the Los Angeles Community College District, was suddenly faced with a 30 percent enrollment decline, he began cutting underenrolled programs and expanding those in demand. The district invested in mass advertising and direct mail, thus reversing the tide and registering an 11 percent enrollment gain in the fall quarter of 1986.

It is clear that public institutions can overcome their built-in dis-incentives for change. Only by staying closely attuned to their student and employer markets can institutions hope to weather the storms of a changing future.

### References

Bluestone, B. "Industrial Dislocation and Its Implications for Public Policy." Unpublished paper, Boston College, 1983.

Bolton, A. Remarks to policy seminar on "Competitiveness, Productivity, and Technology," Sacramento, Calif., Oct. 31, 1985.

California Commission on Industrial Innovations. *Winning Technologies: A New Industrial Strategy for California and the Nation.* Sacramento: California Commission on Industrial Innovations, 1982.

California Employment Development Department. *Displaced Worker Evaluation Report.* Sacramento: Health and Welfare Agency, California Employment Development Department, 1983.

"The Customers Pass the Test—or Else." Articles reprinted from *Business Week* and *Phi Delta Kappan. Education Digest,* 1970, *36* (3), 5-7.

Downs, A. *Inside Bureaucracy.* Boston: Little, Brown, 1967.

Drucker, P. F. "The Changed World Economy." *Foreign Affairs,* 1986, *12* (2), 3-11.

Grubb, N., and Jassaud, D. "Vocationalizing Higher Education: The Causes of Enrollment and Completion in Two-Year Colleges, 1970-1980." Unpublished paper, 1984.

Krafcik, J., and Womack, J. "Comparative Manufacturing Practice: Imbalances and Implications." Briefing paper for the First Policy Forum, International Motor Vehicles Program, Detroit, Mich., May 4, 1987.

Levin, H., and Rumberger, R. *Silicon Chips and French Fries: Jobs in a High-Tech Future.* Stanford, Calif.: Institute for Research on Educational Finance and Governance, Stanford University, 1983.

Levitan, S. "Job Training and Economic Development Policy Seminar." Unpublished paper, Sacramento, Calif., 1984.

Lynton, E. *Employers' Views on Hiring and Retraining: A Nonstatistical Approach to Data-Gathering: Second Annual Report.* New York: Labor Market Information Network, 1979.

Rumberger, R., and Levin, H. *Forecasting the Impact of New Technologies on the*

14

*Future Job Market.* Stanford, Calif.: Institute for Research on Educational Finance and Governance, Stanford University, 1984.

U.S. Bureau of the Census. *Statistical Abstract of the United States, 1986.* Washington, D.C.: U.S. Department of Commerce, 1986.

U.S. Bureau of Labor Statistics. *Employment and Earnings.* Washington, D.C.: U.S. Government Printing Office, 1986.

Wilms, W. W. *Public and Proprietary Vocational Training: A Study of Effectiveness.* Lexington, Mass.: D.C. Heath, 1974.

Wilms, W. W. "Vocational Education and Job Success: The Employer's View." *Phi Delta Kappan,* 1984, *65* (5), 1-5.

Wilms, W. W. "Proprietary Schools: Strangers in Their Own Land." *Change,* 1987, *19* (1), 10-22.

*Wellford W. Wilms is associate professor and assistant dean of students in the Graduate School of Education at the University of California, Los Angeles.*

*California's Employment Training Panel provides a model for meeting the demands of the marketplace.*

# California's Employment Training Panel: Creating Incentives for Change

## Steve Duscha

Training and education will play significant roles in regaining and maintaining America's competitive economic advantage in the world economy. The question for educators is whether traditional public and private schools will lead these efforts or remain on the sidelines as business and labor continue to build their own training systems in corporate and union classrooms and schools.

As political, corporate, and union attention is focused on the need to improve the productivity of the American economy, there is growing recognition of the importance of education and training. Smart, well-trained labor, not cheap labor, will be America's key to international competitiveness, which in turn is the key to maintaining domestic standards of living.

This chapter describes California's Employment Training Panel and how the California program and the principles on which it is based can be applied by public and private schools around the country to help improve economic competitiveness. However, the task will not be easy, because many traditional schools suffer from a competitiveness problem themselves, and the prescriptions recommended here are for a greatly

W. W. Wilms and R. W. Moore (eds.). *Marketing Strategies for Changing Times.*
New Directions for Community Colleges, no. 60. San Francisco: Jossey-Bass, Winter 1987.

different philosophy of how training is managed and controlled and of how its success is measured.

As Wilms (1986) has noted, the Employment Training Panel is based on a clear separation between the provision of broad general education as a foundation for learning and citizenship, on the one hand, and the focused job training that provides survival skills necessary to obtain or continue to hold a job on the other. Basic literacy skills and a general education are the bases on which a thoughtful and compassionate society and a sound economy are built. By the nature of such education, the success of a school in leaving students with a general education is difficult to quantify, although some states are beginning to link students' performance on tests to funding for schools. In contrast, job training has a clear, simple, and measurable goal: a job. If training does not lead to a new job or to mastery of a tangible skill necessary to maintain an existing job, then it has failed both the student, whose economic goals are not met, and the economy, which increasingly demands a changing set of specific job skills to perform its work and successfully compete in the world economy.

The California Employment Training Panel's legal charter is to contract with public and private schools and with business for specific job training. Its focus grows out of its funding from the state unemployment insurance system and out of the business and labor constituencies of that system. Those constituencies demand clear results, as measured by jobs for workers and increased productivity and lower costs for business, but the principles on which the California program is based need not be narrowly applied.

Wilms (1986) also argues that the evaluation of the success of training should be separated from the provision of that training. Under the California statute, the Employment Training Panel evaluates the success of training and disburses funds for training, not on the basis of internal evaluations of program effectiveness but on the basis of a simple test of employment: Did the training pass the test of the marketplace and result in the job (for which the training was designed) lasting for at least a ninety-day probationary period? If it did, then the panel authorizes payment for that student. If not, then the contractor is deemed to have failed in its mission to prepare the student for the demands of work, and no payment is authorized.

## The Risks of Action and Inaction

Should a school enter into such an agreement, with the attendant economic risks? Yes. The economic risks to the educational system, and to the economy at large, of not acting are greater by several measures.

First, at a time when governments at all levels are searching for budgets to cut, schools need allies. Business and labor can and will be effective advocates for the schools if they perceive tangible benefits from them. The benefits business and labor seek are quite specific: Workers need jobs; business needs skilled workers ready to go to work. If business hires the product of a school's training program, that school is a success in the eyes of business. It also is a success in the eyes of the student and worker, who leaves with a job and income to support himself and his family. Arguments about the intrinsic value of any education are of little importance to workers, who need income, and employers, who need productive employees. This is a marketplace test that some schools now meet and that the rest can learn to meet.

Second, few workers now consider public or private vocational schools as significant to their employment. According to the Bureau of Labor Statistics (1985), working people do not report school vocational or job training as important, either for qualifying for or maintaining their present jobs. Asked where they obtained the skills necessary to qualify for their jobs, twice as many workers said they qualified for their jobs in corporate classrooms, through formal company training, as said they qualified through community or technical college programs. Only 5 percent of all those in the labor force cited high school vocational programs as qualifying them for their jobs; 2 percent cited private postsecondary vocational programs; 2 percent cited public post–high school vocational programs; and 5 percent listed community or technical colleges. In the growing field of skill-improvement training for working people, the traditional schools finished even farther behind. Only 5 percent of all workers said they had received skill-improvement training from any vocational program, while 11 percent said they had received such training through formal, company-provided classes. The only schools that play a significant role are four-year colleges, which provide significant amounts of management and professional training.

Third, and most important, a healthy American economy requires high-quality, job-specific training. The new rules of international and domestic competition and the new imperatives of technological change mean that skill requirements to get a job and keep it are changing and will continue to change. Too often, the private sector's solution to changing technology and changing skill requirements is to fire existing workers and hire new ones. Educators understand the importance of education and training to job performance, but many employers do not. Skills are perceived by many firms as commodities to buy on the outside labor market, not as resources to develop from within. Training is considered overhead, not investment, and is viewed as a direct drain on profits. The Personnel Policies Forum of the Bureau of National Affairs (1985) found that only 15 percent of the companies participating in its study reported retraining workers whose jobs were to be eliminated because of technological change. This study also reported that training represented only six-tenths of 1 percent of payroll for the average firm participating in the study, and that the average firm invested only $250 per person trained.

Creative, flexible leadership from public and private schools can help demonstrate to business the importance of training to the economy, to employers' profits, and to workers' paychecks. It is crucial that educators understand the business market for training and how it differs from traditional educational markets, or else they will not be able to compete in those business markets.

Traditional academic systems are generally authoritarian. Teachers teach, and the consumer-students listen and learn. Teachers, with limited administrative supervision, decide what to teach and how to do it and set the standards for measuring achievement and the calendar for delivering instruction.

Serving the business market means shifting to a cooperative model, in which schools share control over education with business and labor. In this marketplace, the consumer is not the student, but rather the firm where the student works or will go to work. Business—with labor's participation, in some circumstances—decides what skills are necessary. Schools can advise and suggest, but they cannot decide. The standards for measuring achievement are not academic, but job-specific. Academic calendars are irrelevant; job schedules are paramount. A cooperative model means schools must share control over training with employers and workers, not by the establishment of advisory councils that meet once a semester, but by an honest sharing of decision-making authority.

## The California Experience

The Employment Training Panel's contracting history yields some insights into what kinds of training business and labor are concerned about today (Employment Training Panel, 1986).

From January 1, 1983, to mid-1987, the panel allocated almost $250 million to business and labor training contracts. All funds allocated by the panel are transferred from the state unemployment insurance system. Each contract is employment-based. The panel begins with employers who want to hire new workers or who want to retrain existing workers in order to avoid laying them off. Each training contract is designed for a specific employer or group of employers. The panel can contract directly with an employer, an employer group, or a public or private school. In any case, employers may select the trainees, the trainers, the curriculum, the method of training, and the standards for successful completion of training. The panel negotiates a fixed fee to be paid for each person trained, hired, and retained on the job for at least ninety days after the end of training. The average contract is for 373 hours of training, at a cost of $2,409 for every person trained, hired, and retained on the job. The panel handles most of the paperwork and monitors the terms of the contract. The following are some general observations drawn from the panel's experience.

*Business Seeks Retraining for Existing Employees.* Contrary to the orientation of most vocational schools, business is more interested in retraining existing workers than in training new employees. Only one-third of the contracts entered into by the panel are for training the unemployed for new jobs. The remainder are for retraining existing employees who are in danger of layoff because of changing technology, changing competitive forces, or sweeping changes in company work processes and systems. Retraining can be necessary for coping with overall reductions of employment within a firm, closure of an office or a plant, or substantial changes in the job duties workers must perform in order to remain on the payroll.

*Training for New Workers.* Training the unemployed for new jobs is important to employers in limited circumstances, in which there is a genuine shortage of skilled labor. Successful entry-level training contracts have been operated by public and private schools for certain aerospace occupations, for machinist apprentices, and for office automation occupations. The success of each contract depends on the circumstances of the local labor market in which the training is offered and on the timing and quality of the training itself.

*Training Is Varied.* Training demands are as variable as the economy and as changeable as business conditions. For example, in one month the Employment Training Panel reviewed proposals from the following:

- A large bank that wished to retrain a group of back-office workers in a new automated system
- Two small banks seeking to prevent layoffs as they merged into one
- A haircutting franchiser seeking to professionalize its management staff
- A department store retraining salespeople in customer-service skills
- Several manufacturing firms retraining people in a variety of job classifications to operate automated scheduling, procurement, and shipping systems
- A cannery seeking to retrain workers to maintain and operate new equipment being installed to meet government safety standards
- A medical laboratory that wanted to retrain employees of another laboratory that was being merged with it
- An expanding drugstore chain that needed new warehouse and supervisory employees

- A medium-sized manufacturer retraining workers in statistical quality control
- A savings and loan association sharpening its focus on customer service and seeking to prevent layoffs
- A nursing home chain retraining office workers to operate a new automated accounting system
- A group of aerospace firms and a group of small machine shops working with a community college district to retrain workers in the operation of computerized machine tools
- A group of machine shops training new apprentice machinists
- A bank retraining computer programmers and analysts to operate and maintain a new computer system
- A commercial bakery retraining workers to operate new automated machinery
- An aerospace firm retraining workers in the operation of new procurement and computer-assisted drafting systems
- A private school teaching computer-assisted drafting and design for a group of firms.

*Corporate Classrooms Are Preferred.* When offered a choice of trainers, business often will select its own training department or consultants, who traditionally are viewed as business training vendors, over public or private training institutions. Organized labor generally backs these business decisions. As Eurich (1985) explains, firms are even building their own internal educational institutions, rather than relying on existing public and private schools. Such developments mean increased competition for public and private schools.

*Training for Small and Medium-Sized Firms.* An important function for schools in the training marketplace is to bring together groups of small and medium-sized employers with similar training needs and to provide training for them. Successful contracts have been operated to train workers in such firms to operate personal computers, computer-assisted drafting terminals, and computer-controlled machine tools. Similar training could be offered to groups of small firms in techniques of statistical quality control and in Japanese, team-style production methods.

*The Importance of Training.* A key challenge is raising the importance of training within firms, large and small. In too many businesses, training is seen as a luxury to be cut back whenever there is a squeeze on quarterly profits. Corporate accountants are not accustomed to weighing the economic benefits against the costs of training, and educators have a responsibility to help demonstrate to business the practical financial benefits of effective training.

## Cooperation

Cooperation among educators, business, and workers is the key to improving America's competitive standing in the world and to maintaining standards of living at home. Some will protest that if this is strictly an economic bargain, government entities like the California Employment Training Panel and public educational institutions have no legitimate role. If training is necessary for business, it is argued, then business will invest in training. If training benefits an individual, he or she should seek it out and pay for it, without government intervention.

Perhaps such a narrow view of public responsibility was true a generation ago, when the only competition the American economy faced was domestic. The United States is now part of a world economy in which domestic economic well-being increasingly depends on the economic decisions of Brazil, Mexico, India, Saudi Arabia, and a host of other countries. To maintain our standard of living in this country, in the face of global economic change, necessarily means a larger role for government in economic affairs. Training is a natural focus for a portion of that new government role.

Government already acknowledges its responsibility to provide basic education as the foundation of future learning. The base of reading, writing, mathematics, and thinking skills must be maintained and strengthened as the schools work cooperatively with business and labor to meet the demands of the workplace.

Such a foundation of basic education is crucial to economic survival and prosperity, but it is no longer sufficient. As international competition grows, America's competitive advantage will depend on how well the knowledge and skills of people are applied to the challenges of the economic marketplace. In California, the Employment Training Panel demonstrates one model for such cooperative programs.

### References

Bureau of Labor Statistics. U.S. Department of Labor, "How Workers Get Their Training." Bulletin 2226. Washington, D.C.: U.S. Department of Labor, 1985.

Employment Training Panel. *Report to the Legislature.* Sacramento, Calif.: Employment Training Panel, 1986.

Eurich, N. P. *Corporate Classrooms: The Learning Business.* New York: The Carnegie Foundation for the Advancement of Teaching, 1985.

Personnel Policies Forum. *"Training and Development Programs."* PPF Survey no. 140. Washington, D.C.: Bureau of National Affairs, 1985.

Wilms, W. W. *Reshaping Job Training for Economic Productivity.* Los Angeles: Institute of Governmental Studies, University of California, 1986.

*Steve Duscha is the executive director of the California Employment Training Panel.*

*In performance contracting, a community college's ability to
make a profit depends on its ability to manage risk.*

# Performance Contracting: Successfully Managing the Risk

*Linda M. Thor*

Millions of dollars, available through federal and state initiatives
designed to address the gap between the skills of individuals and the
requirements of the workplace, are being distributed nationally each year
in employment training contracts. These initiatives are making employment training one of the largest growth areas in education. Community
colleges, as the primary provider of vocational education to adults, should
be major recipients of employment training dollars. However, the intro-
duction of performance contracts into employment training has discour-
aged some community colleges from participation.

Performance contracting is a financing mechanism in which the
provider of services agrees to a payment schedule based on the successful
completion and placement of trainees in jobs for a specific period of
time. Failure to perform results in nonpayment. Performance contracting
thus involves the risk that expenditures will exceed income and that
general-fund monies will have to be used to make up the deficit.

Performance contracting is a relatively new practice in employment training. Usually such training providers as community colleges
are reimbursed for programs on a cost-recovery or cost-reimbursement

W. W. Wilms and R. W. Moore (eds.). *Marketing Strategies for Changing Times.*
New Directions for Community Colleges, no. 60. San Francisco: Jossey-Bass, Winter 1987.

basis. Such methods cover the direct and, in most cases, the excess cost of instruction and do not place the ability to recover the investment in employment training at risk, as does performance contracting. Performance contracting is a response to continuing concern from Congress and state legislatures for accountability in employment training. Through rewarding good performance and penalizing poor performance, it is believed, the overall success of employment training programs will improve.

Nationally, the major funding source using performance contracts is the federal Job Training Partnership Act (JTPA), which is designed to create a public/private partnership to provide employment and training activities to economically disadvantaged youth and adults, dislocated workers, and people with special barriers to employment. JTPA itself is performance-driven, meaning the law requires local service delivery areas (SDAs) to produce measured results for trainees in terms of actual jobs at the end of training, increased earnings, and reduced welfare dependency. Because of this pressure, many SDAs are utilizing performance contracts: If trainees do not get jobs at the end of training, the training provider does not get full payment.

State-funded employment training programs are also utilizing performance contracts, a primary example being California's Employment Training Panel (ETP). The California legislature's intent that all funded training result in jobs for those who successfully complete the training dictates performance contracts.

The financial risk involved in performance contracts varies by funding source. Typically, a JTPA performance contract will allow for progress payments to be paid *and earned* on interim performance measures, such as enrollment or completion of part or all of the training. Final payment is usually received after the trainee has been placed in a training-related job and retained thirty days. ETP, on the other hand, may make progress payments, but payment is not considered to have been earned until the trainee has been retained in employment for ninety consecutive days with a single employer. Progress payments made to trainees not placed and retained must be returned to ETP. This places the contractor at considerable financial risk.

### Advantages of Performance Contracts

Why, then, would a community college want to enter into a performance contract? According to the National Alliance of Business (1984, pp. 5–8), advantages to performance contracts, from a contractor's point of view, include the following.

***Relief From Cost Limitations.*** Performance contracting allows the contractor higher costs in certain categories than are permitted under a cost-reimbursement contract. For example, JTPA limits administrative costs to 15 percent in a cost-reimbursement contract. No breakout of administrative costs is required in a performance contract.

*Opportunity for Profit.* In performance contracts, there are penalties for poor performance and incentives for good performance. Commonly a contractor will estimate programmatic costs and ensure that those costs will be recovered if performance is reasonable or to some standard. Performance that is either better than reasonable or superior will result in a profit.

*Limited Red Tape.* Performance contracting reduces reporting and record-keeping requirements. Since line-item budgets are not part of the contract, costs do not have to be tracked for the funding agency and are not subject to financial audits.

*Focus on Results.* Cost-reimbursement contracts place the emphasis on managing the budget. The financial incentives in performance contracting encourage contractors to focus on results.

In California, by contrast, fifty-eight community colleges that reported having entered into performance contracts indicated that their primary motivations were to strengthen ties to the private sector, to build new student clienteles, and to purchase equipment (Thor, 1986, p. 93).

The primary disadvantage of performance contracting is that if a contractor fails to reach its performance goal, it will be unable to recover its costs, even if the college is not at fault and has operated with integrity and good intentions. In other words, performance contracting places a community college's ability to recover its investment at risk. Whether the college breaks even, makes a profit, or loses money depends on its ability to manage that risk, and a lot can go wrong.

## Problems and Pitfalls

A review by this author of the financial outcome of 129 completed performance contracts funded by JTPA and ETP in California revealed that 36 percent resulted in profit, 43 percent in cost recovery, and 21 percent in loss (Thor, 1986, pp. 73-74). Table 1 presents the financial outcomes of complete JTP contracts as a total and broken down by title. Table 2 presents the financial outcome of complete ETP contracts, as a total and by purpose.

Given that a contractor does not set out to lose money, what goes wrong so that performance contracting can result in such significant losses or in minimal cost recovery?

Contractors can readily identify several dozen common problems encountered in performance contracts that ultimately affect financial outcomes. While some problems are evident, regardless of the funding source, others are more prevalent in specific programs. For example,

#### Table 1. Financial Outcome of Completed JTPA Contracts

|  | Profit Number (%) | Cost Recovery Number (%) | Loss Number (%) | Total Number |
|---|---|---|---|---|
| JTPA IIA | 33(41) | 35(44) | 12(15) | 80 |
| JTPA III | 6(43) | 8(57) | 0(0) | 14 |
| TOTAL | 39(41) | 43(46) | 12(13) | 94 |

*Source:* Thor, 1986.

#### Table 2. Financial Outcome of Completed ETP Contracts

|  | Profit Number (%) | Cost Recovery Number (%) | Loss Number (%) | Total Number |
|---|---|---|---|---|
| ETP New Hire | 4(19) | 8(38) | 9(43) | 21 |
| ETP Retraining | 4(28.5) | 4(28.5) | 6(43) | 14 |
| TOTAL | 8(23) | 12(34) | 15(43) | 35 |

*Source:* Thor, 1986.

while student-related problems (difficulty with recruitment, underenrollment, and higher than anticipated attrition) are among the top-ranked problems, regardless of funding source, employer-related problems are more common in such programs as ETP, because JTPA typically does not have up-front employer participation; rather, individuals are being trained while job developers seek positions for them. ETP, in contrast, requires identification of employers who will hire or retain trainees at the time the contract is approved.

Program- and planning-related problems include inadequate screening and assessment of trainees, schedules that are too long or too short, lack of such support services as counseling, and placing of trainees into ineligible jobs. Other internal problems are inadequate institutional commitment, lack of institutional flexibility, insufficient staff to support the needs of the project, staff changes, and lack of qualified instructors.

Trainee-related problems include difficulty finding an adequate number of eligible participants, higher than anticipated attrition, lack of student commitment, very low reading/writing levels, personal problems, transportation difficulties, and trainees' refusal to be placed in jobs.

Funding source/contract problems are abundant. They include delays in contract execution, minimum contractual wage levels that are too high for successful placement, misunderstandings about the terms and conditions of the performance contract, cash flow/payment problems, changes by the funding source of policies and procedures in mid-project, poor working relationships between organizations, and interference by the funding source.

Other problems, beyond the contractor's control and external to the college, include inadequate employer commitment to hire/retain, changes in the employer's needs, union problems, changes in the labor market, and employers' failure to fulfill agreements.

The lack of shared risk is cited as a problem by many contractors, while others comment on carrying the risk without control. "Think twice," one contractor advises. "The problem is [that] the high-risk parameters are all beyond our control and have little or no bearing on the college's performance as an educational institution." "Be wary," advises another. "Where you cannot hold either employers or trainees accountable, you may well have made expenditures that will not be covered" (Thor, 1986). Finally, simple lack of experience with performance contracting is a major problem in itself.

**Managing the Risk**

How does an inexperienced contractor avoid or minimize these problems? Current literature identifies some basic characteristics of successful employment training programs.

"Knowledge is power," assert Gonzales and Nisenfeld (1985, p. 7). This includes mastering the politics, learning the funding sources' plans and priorities, and knowing the actors.

Successful interorganizational collaboration is key, according to Beder (1984, p. 90). Such collaboration is built around four elements: flexible, adaptive structures; a posture of openness to the external environment; a sense of commitment that engenders trust; and adherence to the principles of reciprocal benefit.

Institutional and top-level commitment are endorsed by Kaplan (1984, p. 83) as characteristics of successful programs. "An extensive program of business and industry training requires support from the college president, board of trustees, administration, and faculty. To maintain this support, the college must establish a community network that includes all constituencies in order to foster a team concept and to ensure that the program has knowledgeable spokespersons and supporters throughout the institution."

However, a successful program needs an identified leader. According to Lapin (1980, p. 10), the leader should be chosen for his or her credibility in academe and skills in program planning, implementation, administration, and evaluation. He or she must be given authority to act and be credible in the eyes of the funding source.

Flexibility and quick response to needs are attributes that must be developed if a college is to be successful in training, according to Kaplan

(1984, pp. 85–86). Beder (1984, pp. 89) agrees: "Organizations that collaborate effectively generally adopt fluid and flexible structures that can adapt well to those of their partners."

## A Planning Process Model

Rose and Nyre (n.d., p. 10) believe that "proper planning and organization guided by both educational and management principles are of utmost importance to the success of employment training programs." They have developed a planning process model that includes seven components: planning, program design, recruitment/identification, screening, program delivery, hiring/retaining/upgrading, and evaluation.

*Planning.* The first phase of the process is feasibility planning. Here, the needs of the employer and the extent of the demand must be defined, and the number of potential participants must be identified. Current information on the labor market is crucial. The second phase is initial planning, during which roles, responsibilities, and relationships are detailed.

*Program Design.* According to Rose and Nyre, "The best starting point for designing a new training program is to determine why current programs are unable to meet the identified need" (p. 4). Then, the basic educational principles of program design should guide the remainder of the work.

*Recruitment/Identification.* A combination of strategies is usually appropriate, ranging from newspaper advertisements to announcements in union halls and referrals from state agencies. Regardless of the methods, material to be circulated must be clear, complete, and accurate to avoid misinformation or misunderstanding.

*Screening.* "The screening of applicants is one of the most critical components of an educational or training program," state Rose and Nyre (p. 6). Gonzales and Nisenfeld (1985, p. 69) agree that "the most elusive, and yet the most significant variable affecting program success . . . is the client." A comprehensive assessment program should be included. "No person should be admitted to a program who does not have at least a reasonable opportunity to complete it," assert Rose and Nyre (pp. 6–7). "This makes good economic sense, but equally, if not even more important, it is only fair to those being considered for the training program."

*Program Delivery.* If all the preceding steps have been effectively carried out, according to Rose and Nyre, success in implementing a training program is "almost a certainty" (p. 8). However, they do admit that problems occur in even the best-planned programs, but that clarity of roles and responsibilities, as well as open and effective lines of communication, can assist in quickly resolving problems.

*Hiring/Retaining/Upgrading.* "The best laid plans and an educationally sound program with a high percentage of completers can fail in the end if the participants are not hired or upgraded," warn Rose and Nyre (p. 8). Sometimes there are defensible reasons for this situation. However, it is incumbent on the program administrators to do everything possible to place completers.

*Evaluation.* Evaluation should begin as early as possible and be ongoing throughout the program. One purpose of evaluation is to determine the program's degree of effectiveness. Another is to monitor the program as it is operating, so that necessary changes can make the program more effective.

Noting that not all programs succeed for exactly the same reasons, Long (1985, p. 40) cites six characteristics common to all good programs.

1. The program meets the needs of the private sector and the clients. Good programs grow out of heavy involvement on the part of private industry and a thorough assessment of the community's needs. They treat each trainee as an individual and thoroughly assess all clients to determine what education and training they need the most.
2. The curriculum of the program is based on employers' input, so that graduates are equipped to meet employers' needs.
3. The program selects participants according to who is best suited to training.
4. Training is as close to real-world situations as possible.
5. Instructors are highly experienced.
6. The program includes counselors' involvement and follow-through. Clients who are having trouble adjusting to the curriculum, the course, or fellow students receive immediate assistance.

"The bottom line, of course," states Long (1985, p. 40), "is job placement. The best training results in jobs."

Survey responses and interviews with experienced contractors provide some specific insight into risk management. As with problems, some of the most common risk-management strategies are present, regardless of funding source, while others are more prevalent in specific programs. Some of the most frequent strategies, regardless of funding source, relate to the presence of a strong project leader, the experience of the instructors and staff, and planning. These are important elements of any program, whether or not it is under a performance contract.

Some risk-management strategies can be implemented before a contract is even executed: planning for attrition, listing multiple job titles to establish training-related occupations, having firm employer commitment to hire/retain, working with multiple employers instead of a single employer, seeking employer input on the curriculum, and planning a short intensive training program. Most important is to make sure everyone involved understands the performance basis of the contract.

"Budget carefully" is the recommendation made most frequently by experienced contractors. "Be sure that steps are taken to ensure that the college gets paid for providing training and services," advises one contractor. "Those costs need to be covered somehow. If a funding agency's performance contracting system does not accommodate this, then perhaps it is not wise to enter into that contract. The key is to avoid a situation where all income is dependent on placement and/or retention on the job, both of which are beyond the college's control."

Other budget-related advice includes budgeting for contingencies, building in a large cushion for noncompleters and employment in non-training-related fields, budgeting breakeven at the minimum expected completion level, and having a nest egg for adequate cash flow until payments are received.

How the contract is negotiated offers several opportunities for successful risk management. Contractors advise colleges to be sure that contract language, conditions, and responsibilities are clear to all parties, to put all promises in writing, to establish realistic goals, to control performance measures as much as possible and set them at comfortable levels, to get the maximum amount of time possible at the end of training to place the trainees, and to contract for superior performance, which allows payment for placement above the goal (if costs are covered by meeting the goal, superior performance placements are all profit). Above all, one must negotiate well and carefully.

How a contractor implements and runs a program can also reduce the risk. For example, overenrolling, assessing applicants and selecting only those most likely to succeed, asking employers to screen participants before they enter training to determine their employability, providing support services and accommodating trainees, and conducting self-monitoring all contribute to successful risk management.

Establishing and publicizing goals was cited by one contractor as the only identifiable variable related to his program's 30 percent improvement in both actual and planned performance in a one-year period. This administrator displays the goals and the current performance statistics throughout the work area, including the classrooms. "The staff always had responsibility for meeting goals," he said, "but before, they didn't have the knowledge of how they were doing" (Thor, 1986).

Contract and financial management is also important. Helpful strategies include combining the project with another funding source, such as apportionment or Vocational Education Act funds, if allowed; withholding nonessential expenditures until cost recovery is certain; making certain that the college's fiscal services unit is capable of meeting the billing and record-keeping requirements; and negotiating contract modifications, as needed.

Passing some financial liability on to employers is a little-used but sound strategy. One contractor indicated that the only reason an ETP contract, which terminated before completion, resulted in cost recovery was that the college had a contract with the employer that called for the employer to cover the actual costs if the project fell apart. An alternative to passing on financial liability is for the employer to be the contractor (in other words, the risk-taker) and the college to be a subcontractor.

Some contractors recommend taking a "total package" perspective before entering into a performance contract. Do an assessment of the culture of the college to see if performance contracting is viable. Is there an affinity for nontraditional education? How attuned is the college to change? What is the relationship between the academic and vocational education programs, and between vocational education and job training? Decide if the college wants to be in the business. Next, determine the advantage of an employment training program to the college. Then look at the practical aspects: Is the staff reasonably tolerant of ambiguity and risk-takers? Is it achievement oriented? If yes, jump in.

Call experienced contractors for advice first. Proceed with caution. Have a good, strong staff. Obtain internal institutional support. Do good planning, preparation, and supervision of the operation. Pay attention to details. Be knowledgeable of the funding source and the employment picture. Ensure commitment of all parties. Expect unreasonable timelines, inconsistencies, and harassment.

In spite of the warnings given by contractors, comments of a more positive nature about performance contracting are heard as well: "With performance contracting, you produce a better product: one you are sure you can place." "In this financially strained time, these contracts are the only way to go to buy equipment and build new programs." " Performance contracting is exciting. It's like being in business. Things happen more quickly than in other college programs" (Thor, 1986).

## The Future

In addition to being a source of revenue, performance contracts appear to provide benefits to the community college beyond the term of the contracts: strengthened ties to the private sector, identification of a new student clientele, revised curriculum, updated faculty, and new equipment. Perhaps this explains why contractors, in spite of previous losses, generally indicate that they would enter into new performance contracts.

Given this inclination, experienced and new contractors need to improve their risk-management abilities in order to avoid future losses and enhance the possibility of cost recovery and profit. At a minimum, the following steps should be taken.

1. Contractors should be prepared to address problems that are beyond the control of the college and that affect performance, such as an

inadequate recruitment pool, changes in the economy, and failure of employers to keep commitments.

2. Contractors should anticipate the burden of serving two masters, the college and the funding source, and the difficulty of addressing dual sets of rules, regulations, and procedures.

3. Contractors should be realistic in their projections of enrollment, completion, placement, employer commitment, and time required for implementation of a contract.

4. Colleges should not rush into performance contracts. Consultation with experienced contractors, adequate planning and careful budgeting, and ensuring the commitment and common understanding of all parties is essential before proceeding.

Above all, remember that the operative word in performance contracting is *performance.* When it comes to determining the bottom line, nothing else is considered.

## References

Beder, H. "Principles for Successful Collaboration." In H. Beder (ed.), *Realizing the Potential of Interorganization Cooperation.* New Directions for Continuing Education, no. 23. San Francisco: Jossey-Bass, 1984.

Gonzales, J., and Nisenfeld, L. *The Job Training Partnership Act and the Community College.* Washington, D.C.: National Council for Resource Development, 1985.

Kaplan, D. J. "Components of Successful Training Programs." In R. J. Kopecek and R. G. Clarke (eds.), *Customized Job Training for Business and Industry.* New Directions for Community Colleges, no. 48. San Francisco: Jossey-Bass, 1984.

Lapin, J. D. "Building and Strengthening Linkages between CETA and Community Colleges." Paper presented at the annual National Council for Resource Development Federal Affairs Workshop, Washington, D.C., December 1980. (ED 245 095)

Long, C. "Tapping into JTPA." *VocEd,* 1985, *60* (3), 38-40.

National Alliance of Business. *Performance Contracting Handbook.* Washington, D.C.: National Alliance of Business, 1984.

Rose, C., and Nyre, G. *A Planning Process Model for Employment Training Programs: Ingredients for Success.* Santa Monica, Calif.: Evaluation and Training Institute, n.d.

Thor, L. M. "An Examination of Risk-Management Strategies in Employment Training Performance Contracts in California Community Colleges." Unpublished doctoral dissertation, Pepperdine University, 1986.

*Linda M. Thor served as senior director of occupational and technical education for the Los Angeles Community College District and managed more than $15 million in performance contracts before becoming president of West Los Angeles College in 1986.*

*This chapter describes elements essential to the success of career-training institutions.*

# Maintaining Links with Local Employers: The Key to Proprietary School Success

*Dean Johnston*

As president of Santa Barbara Business College (SBBC)—a highly successful school with four campuses serving four very different markets from affluent Santa Barbara to blue-collar Fremont—I am often asked to explain how private (proprietary) career-training institutions have survived in the face of increasing financial support for public higher education, especially the community colleges, our chief rival as providers of postsecondary vocational education. In my opinion, the secret of institutional survival lies in knowing the students and their expectations, knowledge that can be derived by means of professionally developed surveys. According to the surveys we have conducted, our students are motivated by a desire to find adequate employment. They choose SBBC because of its excellent reputation for placement, a reputation that results directly from the relationship we have established with private employers. Because of this relationship, which is characteristic of all private career-training schools, we are able to link students with employers.

Our primary goal is to produce graduates who are able to find and keep the kinds of jobs they want. All our programs, placement activities, and other efforts are directed toward this goal. Successful placement

W. W. Wilms and R. W. Moore (eds.). *Marketing Strategies for Changing Times.*
New Directions for Community Colleges, no. 60. San Francisco: Jossey-Bass, Winter 1987.

not only strengthens our relationship with local employers but also increases our appeal to prospective students.

In preparing students to achieve their objective of employment, we expose them to an educational environment essentially the same, physically and psychologically, as that of the workplace. Take, for example, the matter of time. Time is viewed from the employer's perspective, as an economic resource. Our programs are shorter but much more concentrated than those offered by community colleges. Typically, proprietary school students attend class for thirty hours a week over a period of six months. In contrast, community college students usually take from twelve to fifteen hours of classes per week, over a period of two years. The longer hours the proprietary school student spends in the classroom constitute a pattern that closely resembles actual job conditions. In addition, attendance is required at SBBC and may be a consideration when the final grade is assigned. Students are also expected to maintain a professional appearance. In short, we make the same demands on our students as employers typically make on their workers.

**Role of the Placement Director**

Employment of a full-time placement director is essential to the success of a private career-training school. The placement director should have the following qualifications:

- Counseling background, with the placement director expected to help students formulate their goals and accept their limitations
- Ability to motivate students
- Teaching ability
- Research skills
- Public relations skills
- Communication (writing and public speaking) skills
- Ability to follow through on activities
- Interpersonal skills.

The last item is very important, for the placement director is expected to serve as a liaison among the various constituent groups: employers, students, school administrators and teachers, and the community at large. Above all else, the position requires a high degree of dedication and a heavy commitment of time and effort. Obviously, the director's chief objective is the successful job placement of every graduate. To achieve this objective, he or she must be familiar with the local job market, the school's program offerings, and its current students. Each of these responsibilities entails a different set of activities, although many activities serve more than one purpose.

In many schools, for instance, the placement director teaches a professional development course, in which students learn about job interviews, resumés, office politics, and professional attitudes. This classroom contact gives the director an excellent opportunity to learn about current students—their needs, expectations, desires, strengths, and weaknesses. At the same time, students not only master useful employment skills but also see a role model in action. The enthusiasm of the instructor can motivate them in their pursuit of employment goals and can give them the self-confidence they need to reach those goals. Moreover, by inviting employers and graduates to class to speak on real-life work situations, the placement director fulfills the liaison function: Employers get a chance to look over the current crop of prospective employees and to make known their own needs and expectations, while students in turn get a better sense of the kinds of jobs available.

## Building an Employer Network

As mentioned previously, the placement director is responsible for familiarizing himself or herself with the local job market and for making school policymakers aware of employers' needs with respect to training and education. Thus, continual research is an essential activity.

To build a healthy rapport with and establish a network of prospective employers, more active outreach is also necessary. Placement directors have a repertoire of techniques on which to draw. Cold-calling, or simply knocking on doors, is one such technique, especially important when a new school is being introduced to the community. This technique can be broken down into the following steps:

1. Decide what companies to visit by searching the Yellow Pages, the classified want-ads, and business directories.
2. Assemble information about the school and its programs that is appropriate for those businesses (accounting brochures for banks, fashion brochures for retailers).
3. Choose a day when your office workload is light and you can expect to find the appropriate personnel available at each business.
4. When introducing yourself to a new business, be sure that its employees understand the purpose of your visit and that you are talking to the right person.
5. If a position is available, take the necessary information and assure the employer that you will send a satisfactory employee for the job.
6. If no jobs are available at the time, leave the appropriate brochures along with your business card.
7. Follow up every visit with a phone call within a week, and continue to contact each employer on a monthly basis.

Telemarketing has proved to be a useful means of getting job orders from previous employers. This technique involves six steps:

1. Determine which businesses to contact by searching the Yellow Pages, classified want-ads and business directories.
2. Be prepared for every conversation and be sure you have information available to answer any questions that may arise.
3. Introduce yourself and your organization immediately, but make sure that you are talking to the right person before expanding on the purpose of your call.
4. First explain your institution and its programs, then discuss the success of your graduates at other community businesses. Follow this explanation by asking if the employer needs your assistance in filling any positions.
5. If a position is available, make an appointment to meet with the employer to discuss the position and present any possible applicants' resumés.
6. If no jobs are available, try to make an appointment to meet the employer and offer to bring written material about the school and its programs.

Mass mailings can also be helpful, especially in large cities. The placement director should develop an appropriate mailing list. Brochures highlighting the school's various programs should be sent out first and should be followed up with more personal letters, as well as with testimonials from past employers.

More informal contracts also serve to acquaint local employers and the community at large with the school and its programs. Thus, the placement director should attend chamber of commerce meetings, join personnel associations, and participate in various employer-sponsored activities, such as job fairs and training seminars. In addition, a strong affiliation between the school and local employment agencies is beneficial to both parties: The agencies can supply the schools with potential students who require training, and the school can supply the agency with well-trained job applicants.

The placement director should also develop on-campus activities designed to expose employers to the school and its students. For instance, open houses allow employers to observe at first hand the training facilities, equipment, and faculty of the institution. Workshops and seminars give them a chance to demonstrate working methods in their particular fields. Invitations to speak in class or at graduation ceremonies are another way of introducing employers to the educational process. Again, all these activities serve more than one purpose. Through them, students can learn more about work opportunities and about specific employers, and school staff can gain some insight into what employers expect from their workers and can thus make any necessary adjustments in program content and teaching methods.

The school's connections with potential employers can also be strengthened by exposing students to the workplace—for instance, through company tours. A more prolonged and complex kind of exposure can be achieved through the development of a work-experience or cooperative education program, whereby current students receive credit for part-time or temporary employment with participating employers. This arrangement is another example of an activity that benefits all parties concerned. Many employers occasionally find themselves in need of part-time or temporary employees but are unable to attract dependable people with appropriate skills. Through the work-experience program, they can fill these otherwise unfillable positions with young people eager to learn and to satisfy. They also get a chance to sample students' abilities. If a temporary worker proves satisfactory, he or she is often hired on a full-time basis after graduation. Students are afforded the opportunity to find out more about the requirements and rewards of specific jobs, to test their own abilities in the crucible of reality, to earn some extra money, and perhaps to secure long-range employment. In most cases, their exposure to the workplace leads to renewed enthusiasm and increased motivation to complete their programs. Thus, the school itself benefits because its retention rate is improved. Moreover, the student who is financially secure is more likely to fulfill his or her obligation to the school.

**The Placement Process**

To carry out his or her primary function of placing graduates in appropriate jobs, the placement director must be knowledgeable about every program offered by the school and must develop appropriate contacts for placing the graduates of these programs. He or she must also be familiar with each open position and its requirements and must be able to choose the graduate best suited to both the job and the employer. The specifics of the placement process are the following:

1. When an employer calls seeking to fill a position, the job should be recorded on a placement form and filed according to requirements.
2. Job descriptions should be compared with a list of current graduates and their resumés.
3. The employer should be notified of those graduates the placement director feels are suitable for the position.
4. The employer then determines who is appropriate, and the student is responsible for contacting the employer personally.
5. Hiring is the employer's decision, and he or she should notify the placement director of the choice.
6. The graduate is responsible for contacting the placement director after being hired.

Once graduates have been successfully placed, they should be followed up within thirty days by means of a written form, which allows the employer to evaluate them and to make comments. If the employer is satisfied, the school is assured of the suitability of its training. If the employer is dissatisfied, the school can use the employer's input to modify and upgrade its programs. Favorable comments can be used in further job solicitations and in advertising. The placement director can also take advantage of this contact with employers to solicit additional job orders from them. Similarly, the graduates themselves should be asked for their opinions. They are, after all, in the best position to judge the adequacy of their training. Moreover, such follow-up assures them that the school is truly concerned about their success in the workplace.

## Recruitment Devices

Testimonials from employers and from graduates constitute effective advertisements for the school and its programs, but such testimonials must be authentic. Employer testimonials give prospective students some sense of where graduates are placed and what kinds of positions are available to them. The placement director can also use them to solicit further job openings. (See Figure 1 for an example of an employer testimonial.)

Graduate testimonials are an even better recruitment device, since potential students will identify themselves more directly with this group. Successful graduates, presented as qualified and reliable employees, are the best evidence of the school's ability to perform its function. Typically, such graduates take a great deal of pride in their training and in the institution that provided it. Testimonial ads can be very simple. The graduate's name and program appear along with a photo and the name

### Figure 1. Employer Testimonial

Dear Santa Barbara Business College:

It seems your courses have covered all the basics necessary for the business world. If we are using Sheila Cruz as an example of this, you have done a great job!

Sheila is an exceptional self-starter and her skills and attitude will bring her a long way in business. We place great value on the following skills that Sheila demonstrates: typing, business machines, filing, accounts receivable, accounts payable, business math, telephone procedures, and accounting.

I asked Sheila how she felt about the whole learning process at Santa Barbara Business College. She said, "It was very informative, easily understood, and, best of all, they made learning fun!"

Thanks,


Kathy Dyer, Operations Manager
Central Coast Respiratory Services/Medical Supply

of the position and place of employment. Such ads give further exposure to both the graduate and the employer. Often these graduates eventually advance to managerial positions and hire other graduates, to be used in testimonials themselves.

Perhaps the best recruitment device is the school's placement record, which the placement office should make available to the admissions office. After all, students attend career-training schools as a means of gaining employment, and so they have a vital interest in the school's record of finding jobs for its graduates. The placement record also reflects the school's relationship with local employers, many of whom will be familiar to the prospective student. Knowing that the school has linkages with well-known and stable local employers may be the decisive factor in convincing potential students (and their parents) that they should indeed apply.

## Keeping Programs Relevant

The successful private career-training school remains responsive to market changes. This means that its current programs must be kept up to date and that new programs must be developed as the need for them arises.

One excellent way to keep in touch with community needs is to appoint a standing committee to evaluate programs, advise on changes, and assist in the placement of graduates. This advisory committee should consist of employers and graduates who are well acquainted with the school and its philosophy. Every type of employer who might hire the school's graduates should be represented on the committee, which should meet regularly on campus. To be effective, members of the committee must feel that the school values their recommendations and that they are directly involved in the success of its students. Whereas employer members can help the school remain aware of the community's employment needs, the graduate members can bring their experience to bear in evaluating proposed program revisions.

Another way of keeping programs up to date is to make sure that faculty and staff are also kept up to date. It is important to bring employers to the campus, and it is also important to send teachers and administrators into the field. Visits to the sites of the businesses for which the school trains future employees will help educators become aware of what changes have occurred in their fields of expertise and of what employers expect of program graduates. Faculty members can learn about new methods of office management, advances in equipment use, and procedural revisions. They will also have the opportunity to discuss program content with employers. Through these contacts, they can gather course material and recruit business experts for guest lectures. Regular site visits will assure employers that the institution is fully committed to providing the best training possible to potential employees. Such visits can also lead to increased enrollments, because employers who want to update the skills of their current workers will be more likely to enroll them in a school that has proved its concern with quality training.

Trade shows, which are designed to introduce new technologies to the business world, are another resource to be considered in keeping programs up to date. Schools that continually familiarize themselves with the latest advances will be best prepared to provide the training required by the new technologies. Thus, they will be able to develop programs aimed both at the current employees of companies adopting the newest equipment and at students just entering the field. Therefore, faculty, staff, and even students should be encouraged to attend trade shows whenever possible.

In many cases, updating an existing program is not enough. To answer market demand, the school may have to develop new programs. Santa Barbara Business College recently added two new programs, in direct response to community need. The first, in law enforcement/security management, is offered on the Fremont campus, to meet the high security needs of Silicon Valley. Created with input from well-qualified security professionals, and supervised by a former police officer and past owner of a security firm, the program trains managerial personnel for the security field. The second new program, in hotel/motel management, reflects a recent shift toward the service industries in the Bakersfield area and a corresponding demand for management personnel. After deciding that hotel/motel management offered the greatest opportunities for our graduates, we invited experts to the Bakersfield campus for consultation on program development. Faculty and staff regularly attend meetings of the Bakersfield Innkeepers Association, to make sure that the program remains current in its material and to establish the necessary contacts for placement. Both programs have been well received in their communities, and we anticipate no difficulty in placing program graduates.

### Summary

Santa Barbara Business College is approaching its hundredth anniversary. Its longevity can be attributed to its placement record and to its reputation as a provider of quality training, both of which are results of its continued efforts to maintain close ties with private employers. Without this relationship, we could not fulfill our purpose. Such a relationship must serve as the foundation for all career-training institutions. Also essential are appropriate programs, a dedicated faculty and staff, and a qualified and committed placement director.

*Dean Johnston is the president of Santa Barbara Business College.*

*The marketing concept can increase enrollments.*

# Increasing Enrollments: A Marketing Perspective

*Michael K. Brannick*

The environment in which our schools and colleges operate is constantly changing. Consider, for example, the impact of computers on American society. Just a few short years ago, bank tellers did the necessary paperwork manually and returned paper receipts. Today computers, activated by credit cards, complete transactions, update accounts, and issue reports with all debits and credits recorded. Transactions are frequently carried out at locations remote from the bank itself. Scanners prepare grocery receipts, and home computers keep track of household budgets. Such terms as *electronic spreadsheet, program code,* and *input/output stream* have entered the lexicon of most business managers. In short, computer technology has invaded virtually every aspect of our lives.

Postsecondary education is no exception. The number of degrees awarded in computer science increased tenfold over the 1970s. Not only are students taught how to program, operate, and repair computers, but computers have also evolved as an instructional tool, allowing teachers to spend more time on individualized instruction. They are used to keep enrollment statistics, calculate profitability, and distribute payrolls. Computer technology has forever changed the way schools and colleges do business.

Most if not all long-lasting business concerns have found ways to

W. W. Wilms and R. W. Moore (eds.). *Marketing Strategies for Changing Times.*
New Directions for Community Colleges, no. 60. San Francisco: Jossey-Bass, Winter 1987.

forecast and respond to impending change. Adherence to the principles of marketing can make such change less painful and in many instances can create new opportunities for growth. Just as management practices have been modified to allow for developments in computer technology, so must schools allow for the changing needs of their customers, the students.

## The Marketing Concept

Operating a school according to the market concept is simple: Since a school's sole purpose is to attract and keep students, curricula and services that satisfy student needs are successful, while those that do not must fall by the wayside. The essence of marketing is to influence consumers so that they will buy more of the product. For postsecondary education, the challenge is to widen the appeal of the product offered. The focus is sharp, and the customer's needs are paramount.

Complexity is introduced in two ways. First, schools differ in their ability to identify customer needs and to satisfy those needs. For instance, some institutions have attempted to become more market-responsive by shifting to occupational programs, night classes, and extension courses. Second, the number of competing programs designed to meet the same set of customer needs has increased, creating business risk. In 1983, the Council on Postsecondary Accreditation recognized 4,620 institutions, which enrolled over 12 million students and had revenues accounting for approximately 3 percent of the gross national product. Clearly, education is big business, and more players are entering the competitive arena every year.

One useful by-product of adherence to the marketing concept is constant market awareness. The successful marketer makes sure that this awareness is diffused throughout the institution. Because they are continually monitoring the needs of their students, schools and colleges that adopt the marketing approach are able to respond quickly to impending changes and thus to promote enrollment growth. This ability differentiates winners from losers, profitable schools from marginal producers.

*Education as a Product.* In applying the marketing concept to schools and colleges, one must be willing to view the training or curriculum as a product, in the traditional sense. Most of the marketing literature recognizes that good marketing manifests itself in higher sales, greater operational efficiency, or both. In education, this translates to increased enrollments and lower per-student costs for product delivery.

Selling education as a product differs from selling, say, soap, in that the value of education to the customer is not always readily apparent. Clearly, the customer's need to feel clean and smell good drives his or her willingness to purchase a bar of soap, but what drives customers to purchase training or education? Surveys indicate that customers pursue schooling for a variety of reasons: the need to get jobs, to change jobs, or simply to better themselves. The challenge to educators lies in identifying and satisfying these diverse needs.

According to Levitt (1983), there are four kinds of products: generic, expected, augmented, and potential. In education, the generic product is the unadorned curriculum, which differs from other curricula solely on the basis of its subject matter. Thus, courses in computer science satisfy different customer needs than do liberal arts courses. The expected product is the generic course, plus the customer's minimal expectations (the right price, school location, class schedule, and time required to complete the course). The augmented product is the expected product, plus the additional services offered by a school or college (extracurricular activities, job placement, such campus services as cafeterias and bookstores). The potential product comprises everything that is feasible and that might attract and hold customers: what might be done, as opposed to what is being done. For example, a school may determine that transportation services, special payment plans, daycare, and the like will help to differentiate its product from that of its competitors. All these services fall in the realm of potential product, if they are not currently offered.

By identifying the curriculum as a product, educators can more easily adapt it to the changing needs of their customers. Products designed in this manner are more likely to sell, and this consideration should determine what is taught and how it is taught. If a part of the curriculum or an accompanying service does not satisfy a customer need, then it adds needless cost to the product, without any compensating benefit. Prospective students turn to the more customer-directed products of competitors, and enrollment is reduced. For example, because of the general education requirements of two- and four-year college programs, many students enroll instead in the shorter-term specialized programs offered by proprietary schools. The general education requirements are not customer-directed. As a result two- and four-year colleges suffer lower enrollments or higher costs than would otherwise be the case.

*Implementing the Concept.* Marketing conceptualists are attuned to the environment and dedicated to identifying the organization's role and the specific customers it serves. Essential to this process is the preparation of a mission statement, which establishes the organization's operational philosophy and outlines its goals and objectives (achieving profitable returns, increasing enrollments, fulfilling a responsibility to society).

The two basic methods for achieving ever-increasing rates of return while fostering growth are low-cost production and differentiated products to establish high-profit market niches. In the sphere of postsecondary education, low-cost production might entail developing a core curriculum appropriate to several programs, cross-training employees to reduce labor costs, and centralizing purchasing. Organizing to establish market niches might involve offering seminars to business executives during nonpeak instruction hours, targeting high-growth industries for special training programs, and developing curricula with more than one customer application.

According to Kane and Kelley (1983), the implementation of the marketing concept requires seven distinct steps:

1. Determine the marketplace environment.
2. Decide the nature of the business.
3. Identify customer needs.
4. Determine the product and sales strategies.
5. Organize and apply resources.
6. Monitor and measure results.
7. Build feedback loops and reestablish objectives.

As a first step toward achieving profitable increases in enrollments, a school or college must familiarize itself with the environment in which it operates. It must take into account the potential market, the local and national economies, the nature and strength of the competition, and any legal or governmental requirements that may affect it.

The second step involves specification of the institution's objectives (enrollment projections, increase in market share, addition of new curricula, elimination of unprofitable curricula) in formal operational terms and in light of the environmental assessment carried out in the first step. The third step—a detailed examination of the customer—entails identification of need characteristics, buyer behavior, and purchase influencers, as well as an assessment of the school's resources and its ability to affect the customer. In accordance with the objectives outlined in the second step, target customer markets are defined.

After customer needs have been identified, basic sales policy and product strategy must be set. In the context of postsecondary education, this means establishing or modifying curricula; integrating curricula, services, and communications; updating long-range strategy; deciding on sale tactics; and selecting the media to be used to communicate with customers. While it is often assumed that this fourth step, which includes personal selling and advertising, constitutes the whole of marketing, the other steps involved in implementing the overall marketing concept deserve equal attention.

The fifth step, the organization and application of resources, comprises the actions taken by management to ensure that its marketing objectives are met—for example, recruiting and training marketing staff, committing sales support, and selecting channels of distribution. The sixth step recognizes that no organization should institute policies that it cannot measure in terms of cost and benefit. Defining key measures of success, developing a marketing information system, and monitoring its output are necessary activities if a school or a college is to determine the cost-effectiveness of its marketing efforts.

Given the constantly changing environment (including customers and competitors), the plan established in the second step must be constantly fine-tuned and modified. Therefore, the final step involves a commitment to continual review of the marketing plan, in order to determine what needs to be changed. This step also brings the marketing concept full-circle, so that its implementation constitutes a continuous loop in the way the institution does business.

**The Marketing Mix**

The decision to operate a school or a college according to the marketing concept necessitates management of the marketing mix, generally referred to as "the four *p*'s": product, promotion, price, and place. The elements in each of these four variables define its use in creating and keeping customers:

- *Product elements:* brand, design, product line variety, service, style, and warranty
- *Promotion elements:* probably the most complex of the variables: advertising, catalogues, displays, merchandising, personal selling, persuasion, publicity, sales promotion, and public relations
- *Pricing elements:* list price, additional charges (books, usage fees, parking charges), and discounts and allowances (including monthly payment plans and payments by the course)
- *Place distribution elements:* physical distribution (handling, inventory, warehouse storage, transportation), the distribution channels utilized, and the need to evaluate to ensure that they mesh with the customer's and the institution's needs.

While marketing-mix theory applies to all organizations involved in selling goods and services, some variables—and, more important, some elements within those variables—are given more emphasis than others from one industry to another. Educational institutions have typically emphasized product and promotion variables as the way to get customers.

Culley and Lazer (1983, p. 79) contend that the development of an effective marketing mix calls for two basic decisions: Specific target markets must be determined, and the mix of marketing variables that will best serve each must be specified. Market research plays an important role in the latter decision, which should be based on empirical data about variations in customer response to each of the mix variables.

***Product Mix.*** The differences among traditional four-year colleges, community colleges, and accredited proprietary vocational schools are narrowing. It is estimated that almost half the programs offered at the postsecondary level are in vocational fields. As customers seek out the types of institutions that best fit their particular need, loyalty to one "brand" of education over another has shrunk.

In order to compete successfully, an institution must find the appropriate product line variety, accompanied by myriad customer services and backed by an implicit warranty of quality. Thus, some four-year colleges have begun to offer alternatives (executive seminars, continuing education courses) to their traditional baccalaureate programs, while many community colleges and vocational schools are providing services to corporations that have periodic job-training needs, or to government agencies that require assistance in the administration of their training programs.

Changing demographics also affect the product mix. Older people, women, and minorities are enrolling in postsecondary education at increasing rates, and their varying abilities to absorb course content must be taken into account. Traditional curricula and instructional methods are often inappropriate. Consider the ramifications involved in designing a product to meet the needs of three disparate clienteles—inner-city disadvantaged youth, Hispanic immigrants, and older women—all of whom require training to move into, or upward within, the workforce. Clearly, succinct definition of customer needs, and efficient organization to meet those needs, are necessary to ensure that the right products are developed for sale to the customer.

***Promotion Mix.*** As customer needs change, fewer and fewer schools find themselves in the enviable position of turning down applications for admission, and the postsecondary education industry in general spends more and more of its resources on recruiting. Ten years ago, only proprietary schools saw fit to advertise on television. Today, community colleges and, in special instances, four-year colleges are using commercials to get their sales messages across to a generation of high school graduates who grew up with television and who are constantly bombarded with advertising messages of increasing visual and subliminal sophistication.

If it is to be effectively positioned vis-à-vis other products that compete for the customer's discretionary income, education must also be sold through sophisticated means. Thus, the marketing-based school must concern itself with designing communications materials that succinctly describe course content, with promoting the school in the community, and with persuading potential customers that it is superior to the competition.

The purpose of the sales process is to differentiate the product from competing products in terms of its ability to satisfy the customer's needs. Thus, the sales message should be carefully crafted to address the customer's concerns (a requirement that presumes familiarity with the background, educational history, and life experiences of potential customers), and the sales process must be standardized, while still flexible enough to appeal to the uniqueness of each prospective buyer. Sales materials, displays, and merchandising techniques should be integrally designed to avoid confusion and give customers no opportunity for refusal.

Good management of the promotion mix demands that the school be able to monitor the effectiveness of these activities. Advertising is an expensive semivariable cost, and sales staff represent an even more expensive fixed labor cost. Often these constitute new costs of doing business for the school and must be offset by higher enrollments. The goal should be profitable growth, not growth at any cost. Thus, the school must have a marketing information system that shows the costs involved in attracting new students. Ineffective activities should be discontinued. Strong management and quick decision making are also essential to minimize overspending. The school that emphasizes periodic testing of the promotion mix, analysis of results, and rapid procedural changes will find that its marketing costs stay constant or, in some cases, decrease as new efficiencies are identified.

*Price Mix.* Charging what the market will bear and pricing at the margin are simple phrases that describe a very complex marketing activity. Schools and colleges are moving quickly toward an appreciation of how pricing can be used to motivate sales.

One uncommon pricing strategy that has gained acceptance at some four-year colleges is prepayment of tuition at a guaranteed cost, whereby the college attempts to lock the customer in by guaranteeing a certain list price. What is unusual about this practice is the time lapse between the purchase and the actual receipt of goods—in some cases, as long as eighteen years. A more common practice, utilized by many industrial goods manufacturers, is to preannounce future price increases, thereby stimulating immediate demand as consumers scramble to buy at the lower price. Announcing tuition hikes a year or a semester in advance may stimulate some latent demand.

Another pricing technique designed to create customers is unbundled pricing: the separate pricing of elements of the product and its accompanying services. Examples from the sphere of postsecondary education are pricing programs by the course and allowing for service-use fees.

Customer funding is another critical aspect of the pricing mix. Postsecondary students typically rely on loans, grants, or employer reimbursement to help finance education. In setting prices, schools and colleges should be aware of which funding sources their students use. They should aim at enrolling students across a broad spectrum of funding sources, thereby allowing for greater pricing flexibility and reducing the risks associated with overdependence on a single source.

*Distribution Mix.* Innovations in computer-based training have radically altered distribution of the educational product. Gone are the days of reliance on teacher and chalkboard. Today's instructional methods allow the subject matter to be delivered to customers at a pace that maximizes value and retention. Schools and colleges that innovate in this area are bound to realize benefits in higher matriculation rates and happier graduates.

Distribution channels are also evolving, as evidenced by the movement toward branch campuses and campus extensions. As more and more older people with job and family responsibilities pursue postsecondary education, it has become important to locate educational facilities close to the customer's workplace or home, thereby facilitating access and providing greater customer convenience. In deciding where to place its satellite facilities, the school or college must know the needs of the local market, its transportation habits, and its training requirements. This knowledge should guide specific location, selection of curricula, and ultimately the design of the facility itself. By ensuring that all such decisions are targeted to specific customer needs, the school can maximize the benefits inherent in this mix variable.

*Integration of Mix Elements.* No single mix variable can by itself foster enrollment growth. All four variables must work together in a unique combination that satisfies both organizational objectives and customer needs. Management must constantly monitor sales results to ensure that the marketing variables are being used efficiently and effectively. By building feedback loops and encouraging consumer research, schools and colleges can modify the mix as necessary to lower the cost of attracting and keeping customers. As marketing-driven organizations, they must regularly review and revise advertising budgets, train and upgrade their sales forces, and add new products and services.

In such an environment, marketing information systems, which provide all the data necessary for analysis and decision making, represent a cost of doing business. Resources must be committed to assessing customer needs and modifying management strategies. The cost-benefit element of such systems in organizations today proves that schools and colleges can expect to increase their enrollments in excess of these higher operating costs. If no such increase is realized, the institution should assess its current measurement systems before deciding to pursue a non–marketing-based approach. Often a revised measurement system is appropriate to account for changes in the way the institution is marketing itself.

### The Strategic Plan

The strategic plan, which serves as the focal point of an institution's marketing efforts, must be customer-oriented. The crucial question is whether the planning document discusses the particular clienteles to be addressed through each curriculum, the unfulfilled needs of those customers, and the marketing strategy for attracting and keeping them in school. All too many plans present sales forecasts and profit objectives, without adequately considering the customers who will play a role in the achievement of those objectives. The more effective plans recognize that a thorough analysis of organizational, environmental, and customer objectives is necessary for goal achievement.

Organizational goals are the easiest to identify. Their achievement is also easily measured through the balance sheet. Typical objectives of schools and colleges include enrollment growth, increases in key ratios, and greater operational efficiencies. Unfortunately, these goals often lack the customer orientation necessary for long-term success.

Environmental or societal goals present a greater difficulty. The institution's role in society must be defined, and key measures of success must be identified. It is here that questions on the overall role of education arise: What standards should be used in assessing whether a graduate is educated? Is a certain skill level or job competency enough, or should overall literacy be considered? Which is the better measure of success, placement statistics or test scores? These questions touch on some deep philosophical issues. Each institution's strategic plan must outline the direction to be pursued toward the greater benefit of the society in which the institution operates. Measures of these environmental objectives must be predetermined and fair to all competing institutions.

With respect to customer objectives, no school or college should assume that it already knows why its students seek further education. As pointed out earlier, their reasons are diverse and may change over time. Surveys, focus groups, panel discussions, and other well-tested market research methods should be employed periodically, and various clienteles should be compared on their reasons for enrolling, plans and goals, and perceptions of the quality of the education received. Such surveys should be made available to all departments in the school or college, so that each department can be sure that its particular area of responsibility is customer-responsive. When the efforts of all an institution's departments are driven by the same engine—the customer's need—communication among departments can be improved, integration can be achieved, and organizational efficiency can be enhanced.

When a school or a college changes in response to a customer need, the customer should be informed of this change. Students like to know that they are being listened to and that what they say has an impact on the institution. Such feedback can lead to enrollment increases through current customer referrals and a better reputation in the community.

## Summary

Schools and colleges have diverse objectives, and students differ in their reasons for pursuing postsecondary education. By focusing on customers' needs, the marketing approach can help educational institutions achieve organizational, societal, and customer goals and objectives. By providing a common set of assumptions, which all departments can use in their action plans, it can improve organizational efficiency and lower the cost of product delivery.

The most successful business organizations in today's global economy are customer-oriented; they understand that what benefits their customers will also benefit themselves in the long run. Postsecondary educational institutions can similarly benefit by employing the time-tested principles of the marketing concept in their daily operations. Institutions that fail to listen to their customers face a tough future, fraught with shrinking enrollments and declining educational quality. In contrast, market-driven schools will find that the only thing shrinking is space in their classrooms.

## References

Culley, J. D., and Lazer, W. "Developing the Organization's Marketing Mix." In S. H. Britt and N. F. Guess (eds.), *Marketing Manager's Handbook*. Chicago: Dartnell Press, 1983.

Kane, E. J., and Kelley, E. J. "Implementing the Marketing Concept." In S. H. Britt and N. F. Guess (eds.), *Marketing Manager's Handbook*. Chicago: Dartnell Press, 1983.

Levitt, T. *The Marketing Imagination*. New York: Free Press, 1983.

*Michael K. Brannick is the director of marketing research and development for National Education Centers, Incorporated.*

*The Houston Community College System has used marketing research in developing professional training seminars.*

# A 1980s Approach to Planning: The Houston Community College System

*Joyce Boatright, Jacquelin Crowley*

The Houston Community College System (HCCS) has operated in Houston since 1971, providing a full spectrum of educational offerings. With thirty-seven locations throughout the greater metropolitan area and an emphasis on affordable education, HCCS fills a special need as a community agency with capabilities for providing a substantial share of skilled employees for the local economy.

By design, HCCS always has had strong ties with the local business community. Since its inception, the college's primary objective has been to provide occupational and technical programs that prepared individuals for immediate employment in skilled and semiskilled occupations and to provide supplementary training to upgrade present job skills. Not surprisingly, the majority of students who attend HCCS have as their primary objective to improve existing job skills or to prepare for new jobs.

In the early 1980s, in response to the changes in the Houston work environment—a more mobile society, the demands of more sophisticated technology, and the influx of minority groups and displaced workers into the Houston area—HCCS began expanding, not only to provide

W. W. Wilms and R. W. Moore (eds.). *Marketing Strategies for Changing Times.*
New Directions for Community Colleges, no. 60. San Francisco: Jossey-Bass, Winter 1987.

entry-level occupational training but also to make retraining and upgrading programs available to current employees of local companies.

The expansion was timely. From a national perspective, the need for retraining and upgrading America's workforce was evident. In its publication history up to 1982, *Newsweek* had taken editorial positions only four times on national issues. These were race, Vietnam, energy, and unemployment. "Unemployment is at 10.1 percent," *Newsweek* wrote in its October 18, 1982, issue—"but it's due only partly to the recession. A revolution is under way: the smokestack industries are shrinking—leaving millions without the skills to compete in the emerging high-tech economy" ("Jobs . . .," 1982, p. 78).

The college's challenge was to develop a sound marketing plan, so that HCCS could meet employers' changing needs, and to ensure its ability to improve the quality of its services. In the past, HCCS and other educational institutions had been content to let programs sell themselves. In 1983, because of changes in the environment, there was a need for marketing principles to guide the redefinition of institutional goals and program objectives.

As a group, educators did not seem to understand marketing. To some, marketing education conjured up visions of promoters and slick closers who were after sales and easy dollars. To others, marketing was a confusing concept, replete with buzz words like *target segmentation, market share, position,* and *media mix.* In Murphy and McGarrity's (1978) survey of college administrators whose institutions were in trouble because of declining enrollments and spiraling costs, most of the respondents defined marketing as one of their institutions' functions, and 61 percent said marketing was a combination of selling, advertising, and public relations. Only a small percentage described marketing as having to do with needs assessment, market research, product development, pricing, and distribution. In actuality, marketing is a goal-setting, problem-solving process that consists of the same general steps educators are encouraged to follow in any other kind of program: assessment, product (or program) development, promotion, delivery, and evaluation. These are similar to the steps described in contemporary program development by Boyle (1981), Houle (1972), and Knowles (1980).

Kotler (1975) defines the term as follows: "Marketing is the analysis, planning, implementation, and control of carefully formulated programs designed to bring about voluntary exchanges of values with target markets for the purpose of achieving organizational objectives. It relies heavily on designing the organization's offering in terms of the target markets' needs and desires, and on using effective pricing, communication, and distribution to inform, motivate, and service the markets" (p. 5).

**A Case in Point**

Higher education is now confronted with changing enrollment patterns and with changing needs of students. In addition, most institutions face dwindling budgets and increasing costs. Competition among educational institutions for students and financing is intense. These are classic marketing problems. Sound marketing principles can help solve these problems or at least put institutions in a proactive stance in dealing with them.

Despite the focus by HCCS on serving the needs of business and industry, no formal marketing research study sought to bridge the gap that existed between the needs of business and industry and the programs of the community college. Specifically, the study focused on a needs analysis of the Houston business community for professional development seminars.

The overall objectives were the following.

- To identify major companies in the community that could be potential users of professional development seminars
- To determine the image of HCCS as a provider of professional development seminars
- To identify specific professional development seminars that had the greatest potential for successful marketing by HCCS
- To identify ways to communicate the availability and benefits of HCCS professional development seminars.

By 1982, a national push for community colleges to work more closely with business and industry had emerged. The Association of Community College Trustees created the national Business–Industry–Community College Coalition, and the American Association of Community and Junior Colleges initiated its "Put America Back to Work" project. These organizations provided an impetus as well as models for community colleges to address the educational and training needs of business and industry on a local level. For example, nine Texas community colleges, including HCCS, formed the Gulf Coast Consortium. The initial project of the consortium was to inventory its capabilities and publish them in booklet form. While this was a worthwhile project, it followed the traditional approach of putting out the information and letting the programs sell themselves. By 1983, HCCS administrators felt that more contemporary strategies were needed.

The goal for the initial research project was to develop strategies for marketing professional development seminars to Houston companies. The intent of the plan was to demonstrate in an exemplary manner the positive benefits a marketing orientation creates for an institution. According to Kotler and Goldgehn (1981), the benefits should include sensitivity to community educational and training needs, expertise in developing and launching successful programs, capability of creating more effective systems of distributing and delivering programs, awareness of competitive programming, and an ability to create more student, faculty, and administrative satisfaction. The approach would be advantageous for all involved and would reinforce points made by Jackman and Mahoney (1982). Companies in the Houston area would receive high-quality, affordable seminars. HCCS would gain public relations and revenue benefits. Participants would get hands-on training in marketable skills. The larger community would use the business-industry-education cooperative efforts to attract new companies to the region.

## The HCCS Study

HCCS limited its initial marketing plan to developing strategies for marketing professional development seminars from within the sales, marketing, and management division of the Houston Community College System. Business and industry categories were identified for this research by the seminar program specialist, the division chair, and the occupational/technical dean. Business and industry categories were limited to financial, manufacturing, petroleum, retail, service, and wholesale. Companies included in this study were those that indicated they employed 100 or more people. The study did not include companies outside the service area of HCCS.

Data for the initial research were gathered from a telephone survey of 127 Houston-area companies. The telephone survey was conducted by Gelb Consulting Group, Inc., a marketing and management research consulting firm in Houston. The survey, requested and funded by the Houston Community College System, provided the data from which to identify needs among selected Houston companies for professional development seminars and to determine the role for which HCCS was best suited to meet those needs.

The population used for this research was the 1,188 companies listed in the Executive Service Directory, a Greater Houston–area business guide, as employers of 100 or more people and as being within the service area of HCCS. They were listed in the directory in the categories of financial, manufacturing, petroleum, retail service, and wholesale companies. Primary contact persons responsible for purchasing and/or recommending employee training seminars were identified for each firm. A precall letter was sent to all potential respondents on the primary list, along with a Better Business Bureau enclosure, to assure potential respondents that Gelb Consulting Group, Inc., was not soliciting business.

The questionnaire for the survey was developed by Joyce Boatright, director of community relations for Houston Community College

System, with assistance from Judy Jones, project director fo Gelb Consulting Group, Inc.

The survey instrument, composed of twenty-nine questions, was designed to yield data from which qualitative and quantitative analysis would lead to development of strategies for marketing professional development seminars. A pretest of the questionnaire was conducted to determine possible working problems and to ensure clarity. Minor revisions were made. Telephone interviews were conducted from July 8 to July 21, 1983.

Completed interviews were edited, coded, and tabulated. When questions were open-ended, response categories were created through qualitative analysis of the data.

## Answers to HCCS's Questions

Responses to the survey were analyzed to answer four research questions.

1. *Which companies in the community are potential users of professional development seminars?* Only 30 percent of the companies surveyed said they would not consider HCCS for company training, revealing 70 percent as potential users of HCCS professional development seminars. In addition, six of every ten companies had changed how they planned or provided managerial and supervisory training because of the recent recession.

2. *What is the image of HCCS as a provider of professional development seminars?* Almost half the companies considered to be potential users of HCCS seminars had no opinion about HCCS's ability to provide employee training. One-fourth said they thought HCCS was best suited for general management training, while one in ten felt HCCS had strong technical expertise. Of the same group, 62 percent had no opinion regarding types of training for which HCCS was not suited, while 13 percent stated that they felt HCCS was limited in its ability to deliver general management training and was incapable of corporate training. Among the total sample population, only 17 percent perceived HCCS as a second-rate institution, in comparison with its sister universities and four-year colleges. It was surprising to discover, however, that more than half the companies had no opinion about HCCS, because they had no idea of what was available at the college.

3. *What professional development seminars have the greatest potential for successful marketing by HCCS?* General management was the program area most often cited as needed in 1984 by Houston companies. Companies that had sought outside training over the previous two years had contracted most often for programs in general management. Human relations, communication, general management, and leadership were the

programs most often cited by firms that might seek outside resources for previously provided in-house training. If they could customize with an outside provider, at least one in five, and up to 38 percent of the companies, chose communication, general management, and human relations.

4. *In what ways can the availability and benefits of HCCS professional development seminars best be communicated?* Companies depended on informal communication lines, or the grapevine, as an important source of information about training resources. The value of such information was ranked on a five-point scale. Recommendations from other members of one's company were ranked highest, followed by recommendations from other trainers, brochures, and personal calls. No company ranked newspaper ads as very important.

Overall, in considering professional development seminars, companies valued instructors' qualifications, recommendations of others about training programs, and course content as important features. A few firms cited flexibility in scheduling and low cost as benefits they considered most important in choosing outside resources. Since most companies paid all costs directly and in advance for supervisors and managers, flexible payment plans were assumed not to be an important benefit. On-site managerial and supervisory training that could be held during company time appealed to the majority of companies. Nevertheless, 44 percent preferred the benefit of time formats customized to fit individual company needs.

## New Marketing Strategies

Conclusions from the study provided the framework necessary for HCCS to construct new marketing strategies aimed at the business community. The coordinator of seminar programs and her staff assisted all instructional divisions in designing company-specific seminars in supervisory training, time management, coaching and counseling, effective presentations, corporate grammar, and effective writing. Company representatives' responses to HCCS's flexible options were so positive that the college decided to extend its strategies to offer professional development seminars to the general working public. Once a marketing plan and courses had been developed, HCCS was ready to begin its promotional and sales efforts to carve out a market niche and aggressively communicate what the college had to offer. A folder was designed that provided basic information about the seminars. HCCS began a quarterly newsletter and, with a local mailing house, developed target markets, which became the basis on which to build an in-house mailing list.

In addition to promotional materials, HCCS began to network with organizations and associations. Key groups were targeted for active memberships. These included the Houston Chamber of Commerce (with active participation on its International and Domestic Business Committee), Houston Economic Development Council, Houston Committee for Private Sector Initiatives, computer-user groups, American Society of Training and Development, Houston Federation of Professional Women (an organization of professional women's organizations), and Houston Personnel Association, to name a few. Working with these groups not only helped HCCS become better known but also helped the college continue to understand the changing needs of the business community.

During 1984–1985, HCCS opened a new campus, with a business focus. The location for the campus, in the midst of Houston's Galleria area, was chosen because there were over 17,000 companies in the immediate vicinity, and relationships had already been developed with several companies by the director of business/industry development. The focus of the Galleria Area Center is on office automation (particularly in microcomputer applications for business), word processing, technical writing, data processing, and computerized accounting. Because of the array of specialized hardware to support such training, some companies have chosen the center's site for company-specific programs, in addition to their own on-site requests.

The success of HCCS's marketing approach can be seen in enrollments. The Galleria Area Center increased its enrollment by 30 percent in just one year. Systemwide, the number of seminars being conducted for professional training and development has increased, from 14 in 1982–1983 to 178 in 1985–1986. It should also be noted that these seminars do not get state reimbursement; hence, they are "gravy" to an institution in which occupational-technical education is its "meat and potatoes."

**Further Study**

In 1986, HCCS conducted another telephone survey of Houston-area companies. Because of the economic downturn and employee layoffs in Houston, the college included companies that had fifty or more employees. Nearly two-thirds of the companies interviewed (63 percent) had between 50 and 199 employees. These are some of the salient findings.

1. Of the companies surveyed, 64 percent were interested in having their employees take courses, seminars, or training programs. Almost half of them currently provide training for their employees, using outside vendors (organizations outside the company). Conclusion: No single outside provider dominates; the market is still wide open.

2. Of the companies that wanted to provide training to their employees, 38 percent were interested in college credit, 17 percent were not interested in credit, and 45 percent had no preference. Conclusion: Make credit optional. (Also, understand that college credit is not a sales factor to 72 percent of the companies interested in employee training.)

3. Of the companies that wanted employee training, there was diversity regarding format, with 50 percent interested in on-site company-specific training, 73 percent interested in on-campus company-specific training, 33 percent interested in on-campus day classes, 89 percent interested in college placement services, and 84 percent interested in continuing education. Conclusion: Be flexible enough to fit the unique needs of each company.

4. Of the companies interested in employee training, 94 percent provided tuition reimbursement, 64 percent allowed employees to attend classes or seminars on company time, and 28 percent required continuing education and/or professional development for advancement. Conclusion: Companies are willing to pay the bill for employee training.

5. Companies were asked specifically to name the colleges, community colleges, and organizations in the Houston area that could best meet their employees' needs. A follow-up question was used: "What other schools come to mind?" Of those who responded, 26 percent named HCCS first (19 percent named HCCS in the follow-up), and 13 percent named one of the other eight community college districts in the Gulf Coast Consortium. Conclusion: More and more Houston-area companies think of community colleges first as a "best fit" when they are choosing continuing education for credit or noncredit.

As a result of the initial marketing study, HCCS now has a planned approach to developing its services to the business community. The Office of Business–Industry Development has been organized, and human resources have been reassigned to create the staff support services for a total marketing effort. The Office of Business–Industry Development coordinates seminar program activities, cooperative education, and small-business programs, working particularly with occupational-technical program areas to market and coordinate all activities with business and industry. The Office of Business–Industry Development is assisted by a strong advisory committee composed of Houston company representatives, and it is developing an overall strategic marketing plan for each instructional program area. The advisory committee is representative of the sectors that are the backbone of Houston, including city government, the economic development council, energy companies, banks, and small businesses.

HCCS has found that professional training and development seminars are a valid way to approach new learning opportunities for the adult business community. Networking within organizations and associations has proved to be a valuable way to build credibility in the training community and to identify key resources to assist in accomplishing objectives. It is also very important to know one's markets—not only to identify them on paper, but also to meet with representatives and discuss their needs. Finally it is essential to do what one says one is going to do.

# References

Boyle, P. G. *Planning Better Programs.* New York: McGraw-Hill, 1981.

Houle, C. O. *The Design of Education.* San Francisco: Jossey-Bass, 1972.

Jackman, M.J.G., and Mahoney, J. R. *Shoulders to the Wheel: Energy-Related College/Business Cooperative Agreements.* Washington, D.C.: American Association of Community and Junior Colleges, Energy Communications Center, 1982.

"Jobs: Putting America Back to Work." *Newsweek,* October 18, 1982, pp. 78–88.

Knowles, M. S. *The Modern Practice of Adult Education: From Pedagogy to Andragogy.* Chicago: Follett, 1980.

Kotler, P. *Marketing for Nonprofit Organizations.* Englewood Cliffs, N.J.: Prentice-Hall, 1975.

Kotler, P., and Goldgehn, L. A. "Marketing: A Definition for Community Colleges." In W. A. Keim and M. C. Keim (eds.), *Marketing the Program.* New Directions for Community Colleges, no. 36. San Francisco: Jossey-Bass, 1981.

Murphy, P. E., and McGarrity, R. A. "Marketing Universities: A Survey of Student Recruiting Activities." *College and University,* 1978, *53* (3), 249–261.

*Joyce Boatright is director of community relations in the Houston Community College System.*

*Jacquelin Crowley is associate director of business and industry development in the Houston Community College System.*

*Market research allows educators to follow the student market and respond to trends.*

# Student Recruitment: A Market Research Primer

## Richard W. Moore

Demographic change is reshaping the markets served by community colleges and proprietary schools. The number of traditional students coming to institutions directly out of high school is already in steep decline. In the 1980s, for the first time in American history, less than 30 percent of the population will be under twenty years old. As a result, the number of high school graduates will decline, from 3 million in 1980 to 2.4 million in 1990. This trend will continue until 1998, when the children of the Baby Boomers begin to graduate. Meanwhile, the 70 million people who make up the Baby Boom generation are reaching middle age, creating a tremendous demand for retraining and continuing education.

Other trends further complicate the picture. While the general population is aging, the ethnic mix of youth is changing radically as the result of varying fertility rates among different ethnic groups. Minorities now account for half the public school enrollments in California and for 46 percent in Texas. Half the states have public school enrollments that are at least 24 percent minority. After increasing steadily for thirty years, high school graduation rates have dropped, from 79 percent in 1980 to 73 percent in 1985. The impact of these trends will vary significantly from region to region and city to city, but most colleges can expect continued change in their communities for the next decade.

W. W. Wilms and R. W. Moore (eds.). *Marketing Strategies for Changing Times.*
New Directions for Community Colleges, no. 60. San Francisco: Jossey-Bass, Winter 1987.

These demographic changes are already creating two consequences for two-year institutions: increased competition for students, and shifting educational needs. To cope with this new environment, administrators need to think about potential students as consumers with an increasing number of options in the postsecondary educational market. Community colleges and proprietary schools now compete not solely with other accredited two-year institutions but also with university extensions, weekend colleges, the military, and a host of unaccredited or nonformal institutions.

To survive in this competitive market, institutions must begin to think in market terms. To understand the market and your position within it, you must be able to answer the following key market questions:

- Who are our current students?
- How can they be described in terms of the market?
- What is the potential of our entire market?
- Which segments of the market are we reaching successfully?
- Which segments are we not reaching?
- With which institutions do we compete?
- How do potential students view our institutions?

The purpose of this chapter is to illustrate how proprietary schools and community colleges around the country have used market research techniques, previously restricted to the business world, to answer these questions and to make innovations to respond to market changes.

## Identifying Marketing Problems

The first step is to begin thinking about the institution's service areas in marketing terms. A good way to start is with a marketing problem inventory. To conduct a marketing problem inventory simply means to have representatives from different departments (admissions, financial aid, academics, and so on) develop a list of problems, as they perceive them. Many of these problems may not be stated in marketing terms. For example, financial aid administrators may note that slow turnaround on loan applications discourages applicants. Others may note parking problems or a lack of sections in popular courses.

Correlating these lists will allow the institution to identify potential problem areas. The second step, after identifying problem areas, is to determine what information is needed to measure the extent of the problem and ultimately to solve the problem. For example, one community college faculty member observed that, despite the fact that the college served an area with a large number of single parents, few single parents seemed to be enrolling. Obviously, information was needed on how many single parents were actually enrolled in the institution, compared to the number in the community, to determine if this observation was valid. More in-depth data on how single parents perceived the college, and on why they did or did not enroll, were also needed to understand the phenomenon.

The following sections will identify some market research strategies that have been used to answer these types of questions and many more like them.

**Know Whom You Have**

A suburban community college carefully tracked its enrollment each term. It recognized that evening and part-time enrollment was growing rapidly, but that full-time day enrollment was declining. A committee was formed to see what could be done to increase full-time day enrollment. The committee recognized immediately that although it had some general perceptions about day students—they were younger and more likely to take academic programs—there was incomplete understanding of what separated them from the evening students. A survey was conducted to compare full-time day and part-time evening students. The results identified a number of key differences. Full-time day students were likely to have recently left four-year institutions or two-year colleges. They were far more dependent on financial aid to cover their costs and had less specific goals for education. With these differences in mind, the college began actively recruiting, sending direct-mail pieces to young people who had graduated from local high schools one to three years before. The college streamlined its financial aid processing and provided additional time for counseling these applicants when they visited the campus for admissions interviews. The results were increased full-time day enrollments.

The most basic market information that every institution should have is a comprehensive database that provides complete descriptions of the current student body and of important subgroups within it. Most institutions collect reams of data on students. Financial aid departments have data on students' financial situations. The registrar has information on grades, other schools attended, and academic standing. Unfortunately, these data are often collected for accounting purposes, or to comply with government regulations. As a result, institutions are often unable to merge what they have into one effective research database.

Few institutions can empirically describe how the demographics of students vary from program to program. Further, very few institutions track data on the students' behavior as consumers of postsecondary education. Could your institution answer these questions?

- How did your students learn about your institution?
- Do older students learn about your institution from different sources than younger students do?

- How do the demographics of students in vocational programs compare to those of students in academic programs?
- Did students consider other institutions before enrolling at your college? Which ones?
- Why did students select your institution and particular programs over competing institutions?

To compensate for the limits of existing systems, many institutions periodically survey their student bodies to gather these types of marketing data. These surveys typically include items on student demographics, previous education, media habits, reasons for selecting school and program, perceptions of competing institutions, commuting patterns, methods of financing education, satisfaction with college and program, and academic standing.

Other institutions use one of two national services that conduct student surveys to gather this type of information: the Cooperative Institutional Research Program's (CIRP) Freshman Survey, which annually surveys entering freshmen and compares an institution's data to national norms for similar institutions; and the Proprietary Market Information System (ProMIS), which is specifically designed as a market research survey for proprietary schools.

A key to analyzing descriptive data on current students is to segment your student body into a number of logical subgroups and then compare them. Segments should be constructed to isolate groups that logic and experience indicate will behave differently as consumers. For example, one proprietary business college conducted a survey of its current student body and decided to segment the population into four age-sex groups: men under twenty-five, men twenty-five and older, women under twenty-five, and women twenty-five and older. This comparison revealed that each of these four groups chose programs for very different reasons. Younger men and women chose programs because of intrinsic interest in the field and because the field offered long-term career opportunities. Older men and women chose programs because of immediate opportunities for employment and high wages. Once the college understood these differences, it designed publications that were aimed at each age-sex segment. Admissions representatives were trained to respond to the unique interests of each group. Student populations can also be segmented by ethnicity, income categories, previous educational experience, or geography, depending on the problem that is being studied. Access to complete data on the current student population is the key first step to more sophisticated market research.

**Know Whom You Do Not Have**

Most community colleges and proprietary schools serve limited geographical markets. This makes understanding the market relatively simple. The easiest way to describe an institution's market is to analyze the U.S. Census data for that area. Census data provide information on most demographic variables, such as age, sex, ethnicity, income, and education, as well as home ownership, distance commuted to work, and other information. Often these data are available from city or county planning departments.

Two companies—Donnely Marketing, a Division of Dun & Bradstreet, and National Decisions Systems—offer census data that have been enhanced by taking the 1980 U.S. Census data and estimating figures for the current year, and then projecting trends forward for five years.

At the most basic level, these data will show you the characteristics of people in your market. For example, they reveal how many people are in the traditional college-age population and what percent of the population earns less than $10,000 a year. By looking at different geographical areas within the market, it is possible to identify where different segments are.

*Measuring Market Penetration.* These types of data become more useful when merged with data on existing students, to identify areas in the market where the institution is successfully reaching students.

Figure 1 shows the type of analysis that can be produced when U.S. Census data are merged with data from a student survey. In this case, a student survey had identified the characteristics of students and their home zip codes. The number of women students aged eighteen to twenty-four from each zip-code area was identified. Then, from the U.S. Census data, the number of women aged eighteen to twenty-four in the general population from each zip-code area was calculated. To measure market penetration, the number of students was divided by the total population aged eighteen to twenty-four in each zip-code area. The results were plotted on a map clearly depicting the pattern of penetration with the city.

The next step in this particular study was to match the levels of penetration with the demographic characteristics of the zip-code area to identify which segments of the market the college was reaching or missing. The analysis showed that the college had high levels of penetration in low-income, predominantly white areas, with lower penetration in middle-class and minority areas.

Ultimately, analysis was used to target direct-mail advertising and other recruitment resources on areas where penetration was low, but where there were large numbers of people in the target market segment— women aged eighteen to twenty-four. By targeting its marketing resources accurately, the college increased enrollments and reached areas of the community it had not served in the past.

*Moving from Description to Prediction.* Once an institution understands its current market penetration, it can use that information to make predictions that address such key questions as these:

Figure 1. Market Penetration by Ethnic Background and Zip Code

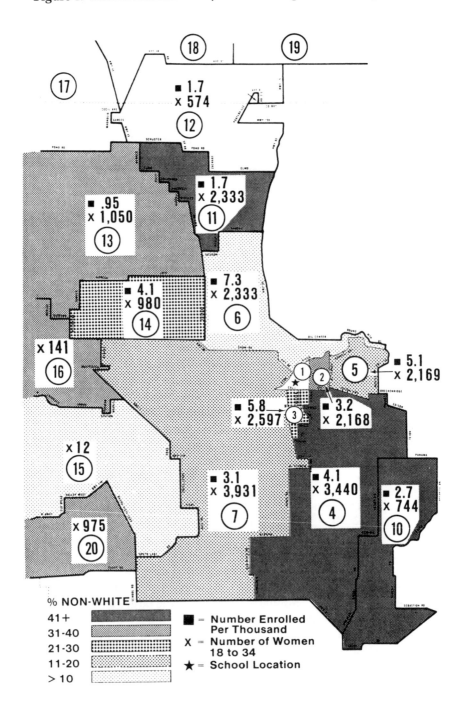

- How many students will enroll next year? In five years?
- How will the characteristics of the community around the campus change?
- What would be the best location for a branch campus?
- How many students are likely to enroll at that campus?

The databases described previously take the 1980 U.S. Census data, update them for the current year, and project them forward for five years. These updated and projected data can be combined with data on current market penetration to make predictions.

A database capable of making predictions can be created by extracting the U.S. Census database predicted population demographics for each unit (zip-code area, census tract, and so on) in the college's market. When these data are merged with data on current enrollments, a database capable of making a variety of predictions is created. The two examples below illustrate how such a database can be put to work.

***The Case of UR Business College.*** The business college in the example illustrated by Figure 1 needed an estimate of its future enrollments in order to develop a long-range organizational plan. The college knew that its primary market was women aged eighteen to twenty-four. From its previous study, it also knew what its current market penetration was in each zip-code area in the market. To predict what its enrollments would be in five years if its market penetration remained the same, it applied the current penetration figures (in enrollments per thousand—women aged eighteen to twenty-four) to the five-year population projections. This analysis produced a predicted enrollment figure for each zip-code area and a predicted enrollment figure for the entire market. The results showed that if the college maintained its current market penetration, enrollments would fall 8 percent in the next five years.

The cause of the decline was simply that the number of women in the targeted age group was decreasing rapidly. Further analysis showed that the pattern was not uniform. The number of these women would decline more steeply in some zip codes and actually increase in others. Overlaying the changes in the number of these women with the predicted ethnic mix of the zip codes made it clear that the decline would be in predominantly white and black zip codes, and that there would be increases in the areas within this market that had large numbers of Hispanics.

After reviewing the research, the college realized that to grow or even maintain its current size, it would have to either increase market penetration or reach new markets. The school chose to begin recruiting students more aggressively in the growing Hispanic community and to add evening programs designed to appeal to women over twenty-five, a market segment predicted to grow substantially in the next five years.

Once these decisions were made, planners needed to estimate how many students these new programs would produce. To estimate enrollments for these programs that did not yet exist, researchers developed three scenarios, each assuming a different level of market penetration (measured in enrollments per thousand—women aged twenty-five to forty-five). These three scenarios created low, medium, and high enrollment estimates, which the planners then used in estimating costs, developing materials, and ultimately marketing programs. Since the analysis was done on a zip code–by–zip code basis, it also allowed the planners to identify high-potential areas within the market for intensive recruitment.

*The Case of City Junior College.* City Junior College was a rapidly growing junior college on the north side of a large city. By plotting the location of enrollments on a zip-code map, the president of the college realized that he was drawing a substantial number of students from the relatively distant south side of the city. His immediate response was to call a real-estate agent and begin to look for a site for a south-side branch campus. The real-estate agent found two potential sites. The president was then faced with the problem of choosing between the sites. At the same time, the dean of admissions raised the issue that the south-side branch campus might "cannibalize" the main campus by competing with it for students.

To decide whether to go forward with the new branch, the president needed to predict what the enrollment consequences of opening the branch campus would be. A study was designed to measure the market potential of each site and to estimate the degree to which the new branch campus would compete with the main campus for students.

First, the markets for the two proposed campuses were defined as two groups of zip codes. The demographic data, including five-year projections, were gathered for each zip code in each of the two potential markets. Then, on the basis of penetration rates around the existing school site, which were substantially higher than the current, relatively low-penetration rates in the branch market, enrollment estimates were made for each site. As the final step, the number of students currently enrolled from each of the two proposed branch markets was identified and matched with corresponding U.S. Census data to estimate current market penetration. If these students all went to the new branch, the number of students that would be lost to the main campus over the next five years could be estimated.

The results of the analysis found that one site clearly had more potential. By opening the new branch, the college would experience a 27 percent net increase in enrollments over five years. The enrollment at the main campus, however, would decline about 4 percent, as the college lost students from the south-side market to the branch campus. With this information, planners were able to develop programs and facilities based on realistic estimates of future enrollments at both sites.

## Know Your Competition

You need to understand your market position. This requires up-to-date information on competing institutions and an understanding of how your students perceive your institution in comparison with competing institutions. To develop a sophisticated understanding of your market position, you need three types of data: a list of institutions with which you compete; the hard facts on competitors' enrollments, program offerings, and facilities; and an understanding of competitors' marketing strategies.

*Competing Institutions.* Simply identifying the institutions with which you compete can be eye-opening. One community college had always assumed it competed primarily with other community colleges in the area and with local proprietary schools. To gain a better understanding of its competition, the college asked new applicants one fall to name the other institutions they had considered. To the surprise of the entire admissions department, the most common responses were the local four-year state university and the military.

*Hard Facts.* Once an institution has a clear idea of whom it competes with, it needs to develop an annual profile of the competition. There is an abundance of publicly available data on most educational institutions, particularly on public institutions, which must submit large amounts of information to state and federal agencies. Certainly, for most institutions, basic facts on enrollment, program offerings, accreditation, and facilities are available in the institution's catalogue or in college directories. Keeping this type of data on each competing institution will provide both a basic overview of the market and a handy resource for planning and marketing.

*Competition's Marketing Strategies.* Developing a qualitative understanding of your competition's market strategies is an important part of market research. A variety of methods can help you gather qualitative data on your competition. The most direct way is to visit competing institutions, collect their publications, and review them. A more subtle strategy, called the "mystery shopper" strategy in business, is to have a staff member of your institution go through the recruitment and application process at the competition and report the experience.

This type of qualitative data will help you find out how the competition is presenting itself to the potential student. What comparisons, if any, are they drawing between themselves and your institution? It will give you first-hand experience with how they treat their applicants. Are they friendly and concerned, or distant and bureaucratic? Are applications processed promptly? What aspects of their offerings do they emphasize? How good are their publications?

## Understanding Applicants' Perceptions

In student recruitment, applicants' perceptions of your institution are often more important than the facts. Focus groups and applicant surveys provide two research methods for getting systematic data on how your institution is perceived in comparison with others.

Focus groups are part of a qualitative market research method that involves conducting open-ended interviews with groups of eight to twelve participants. Each focus group is usually homogeneous, representing one market segment, such as recent male high school graduates or employed women over twenty-five. The group should be led by an experienced facilitator who has prepared a short list of questions to guide the session. Focus groups are often held in specially designed facilities with one-way mirrors, so that representatives of the institution can observe the group. Often audio- or video-tapes of the session are made, to be analyzed after the session.

Calder (1977) identified three purposes for which focus groups can be used: to generate hypotheses for further research, to help researchers understand the causes behind behaviors or attitudes that have been identified in quantitative research, and simply to help researchers develop intuitive understanding of groups' experiences and opinions.

*The Case of BB College.* BB College, a private two-year college in the suburbs of a major metropolitan area, had attempted to learn more about its market position by conducting an extensive survey of its existing students. Through the survey, it identified two questions needing additional study: Why did few older women choose to attend, and why did applicants who were recent high school graduates choose to attend other, similar two-year colleges in the area?

To get data to answer these questions, the college hired a research firm to conduct four focus groups. Two groups were made up of older women who were considering returning to school, and two groups were made up of recent high school graduates who had chosen competing institutions. Each group met for two hours. The research firm provided an experienced facilitator, who led the groups' discussion of the guiding questions, which were developed jointly by BB College's admissions staff and the research firm. The research firm analyzed the audiotape of the sessions and provided policy recommendations in a report.

Analysis of the groups' comments found that older women viewed the college as being of high quality and as an appropriate place for someone right out of high school, but as a place where an older student would be uncomfortable. Despite aggressive marketing of a part-time evening program, the participants also believed the college offered only full-time day programs.

Younger students who chose other colleges did so because they viewed BB College as a high-quality institution, but too difficult for them, as well as expensive. They were drawn to competing institutions that offered more personalized attention in the admissions process and that were perceived as less expensive.

Given the results of these focus groups, the college repositioned itself in the market as an institution prepared to meet the unique needs of older working women, by creating an evening institute with a name and identity separate from that of the more traditional day program.

To compete more effectively for full-time day students, the college provided retraining for admissions staff, to make sure that they gave personal attention to each applicant. In reality, the college was no more expensive than similar competing private institutions. This point was emphasized in admissions presentations and in publications, to combat the image of an expensive college.

Surveys of applicants who do not enroll are another method for developing an understanding of your market position.

***The Case of CMR College.*** CMR is a large two-year business college in the downtown section of a large city. Aggressive recruitment and marketing had increased the number of applicants to the college dramatically, but the increased applications had not led to increased enrollments. To understand what was behind this phenomenon, CMR decided to conduct a phone survey of a sample of applicants who had not enrolled.

An analysis of the survey's results showed that 71 percent of the applicants who did not enroll at CMR enrolled at other institutions, most often at local community colleges. Smaller groups chose other private two-year colleges and public four-year colleges. The reasons they did not select CMR varied from group to group. Blacks did not select CMR because they perceived it as too expensive, while whites did not enroll because they disliked the downtown location.

To increase the proportion of applicants who would enroll, the college developed strategies to meet these two objectives. A special publication that features the advantages of a downtown location, with information about how to commute, was developed and distributed to applicants from outside the central city. Applicants were also given additional information about the availability of financial aid, to reduce the shock experienced by applicants upon their being confronted with tuition costs.

## Conclusion

Demographic change, shifting student preferences, and increased competition will be affecting all two-year colleges, public and private alike. To succeed in this shifting environment, institutions must respond quickly to the changing student market. Market research techniques, which have traditionally been used by business, provide educators with tools that allow them to systematically follow the market and respond promptly to changes as they emerge.

**Selected Bibliography of Market Research in Education**

Constantine, K. K. *An Annotated and Extended Bibliography of Higher Education Marketing*. Chicago: American Marketing Association, 1986.
This lengthy bibliography includes 218 items published between 1980 and 1985. Annotations are included for 169 of the citations. Entries are cross-indexed and cover all aspects of marketing and student recruitment. There are 74 entries in the area of "Market Research and Information Systems."

Kotler, P., and Fox, K. F. *Strategic Marketing for Educational Institutions*. Englewood Cliffs, N.J.: Prentice-Hall, 1985.
This book covers the basics of marketing for all types of educational institutions: public and private, elementary, secondary, and postsecondary. Material is presented in six sections: understanding marketing, the elements of marketing, planning marketing, establishing the marketing mix, applying marketing, and evaluating marketing. The focus of the book is theoretical, but it does include numerous examples.

Lay, R. S., and Endo, J. J. *Designing and Using Market Research*. New Directions for Institutional Research, no. 54. San Francisco: Jossey-Bass, 1987.
This sourcebook includes chapters on institutional images, assessing the market for new programs, describing patterns of competition, market positioning, balancing price and value, market segmentation, and developing a marketing plan. Most of the focus is on traditional four-year colleges and on national and regional markets, but many chapters provide detailed descriptions of how various market research techniques can be applied to higher education.

Topor, R. *Marketing Higher Education: A Practical Guide*. Washington, D.C.: Council for the Advancement and Support of Education, 1983.
This is a brief and excellent hands-on guide to all aspects of marketing a postsecondary institution. The focus is on traditional four-year colleges. The book includes brief case studies that help explain the concepts. Worksheets to help the readers assess their own institution are available in each chapter.

**Reference**

Calder, B. J. "Focus Groups and the Nature of Qualitative Marketing Research." *Journal of Marketing Research*, 1977, *14*, 353–364.

*Richard W. Moore is the executive director of Training Research Corporation.*

*Public relations can win community support for the college.*

# Public Relations
# and Marketing

*Daniel D. Savage*

In the decades ahead, postsecondary educational institutions face life-threatening challenges as they vie with one another for enrollments and for public support. The position of the community college is especially tenuous. Its vocational programs have been criticized on the grounds that they fail to meet the current needs of students and employers. They are accused of having lost touch with local labor markets and of lacking the capacity to respond quickly to market forces. In many cases, funding for community colleges has been reduced, and some institutions have been forced to raise tuition or to impose it for the first time.

Given recent cuts in federal student aid (and talk of even deeper cuts in the future), prospective students have become more careful shoppers. Substantial numbers who would previously have enrolled in community colleges are attracted by the shorter, more focused programs of proprietary vocational schools. These schools—driven by the profit motive, and free of the bureaucratic inertia that characterizes too many community colleges—tend to maintain close contact with local markets and thus to be aware of changes in employers' needs and job requirements. They have curricular flexibility, allowing them to add or drop courses as necessary. Many of them also have good reputations for successful job placement. In short, proprietary vocational schools seem to be

W. W. Wilms and R. W. Moore (eds.). *Marketing Strategies for Changing Times.*
New Directions for Community Colleges, no. 60. San Francisco: Jossey-Bass, Winter 1987.

strong in the very areas where community colleges are viewed as weak. Thus, they have become formidable contenders in the postsecondary vocational arena.

Survival in an increasingly competitive environment requires, first of all, that providers of vocational education recognize that the world in which they exist is not static. The character of the local school district changes: Groups of people move into or out of the district; new businesses are established, and some older businesses go under or drastically alter their operations; rival institutions open up, close down, or modify their programs. At the same time, other kinds of changes are taking place: New generations of high school graduates, with different values and different aspirations, enter the labor market; nontraditional groups (for example, Hispanics, single mothers) seek training that will help them improve occupational status; technological advances affect the nature of work itself, resulting in new skill requirements.

In view of the dynamics of the situation, the most successful vocational institutions will be those that, through market research, monitor changes in students' and employers' needs as they occur. They must also be prepared to respond to those needs, introducing new curricula in accordance with student and employer demand and eliminating programs that no longer serve specific functions. But awareness and response are not by themselves enough. The institution must also make the community aware of the relevance of its vocational programs and must garner the community support required if it is to remain financially sound and educationally flexible. It is here that public relations can make a contribution.

Developing an effective public relations component has long been an instinctive concern of community college leaders, who realize that close ties to the surrounding community are a distinctive feature of their institutions. All too often, however, the public relations effort amounts to little more than conveying such information about the institution's mission, goals, and programs as the chief executive officer (CEO) deems appropriate. The starting point of the institution's conversation with the public is the ethos of the institution itself—usually a reflection of the CEO's own deeply held values and beliefs. The effectiveness of the public relations effort is measured in terms of the quantity and quality of the activities undertaken. Little attention is given to the question of whether these activities have indeed increased understanding and won support for the community college.

A new approach to public relations is required. The starting point of the conversation must be the attitudes and values of the institution's constituencies, including prospective students and local employers. Assessment must focus on changes in those attitudes and values. A carefully crafted strategy, based on an accurate reading of current public interests and understanding, is the key to creating an effective public relations program. The role of the public information officer (PIO) must be clearly defined, institutional resources must be organized and mobilized, and a long-term plan must be developed. In the remainder of this chapter, each of these points is discussed in turn, and examples of proactive public relations are given.

## The Role of the PIO

With the growth of public relations programs at the baccalaureate and master's levels, more and more young people who take jobs as college PIOs are professionals whose experience is limited to the field of public relations. In contrast, older PIOs typically have degrees in journalism, plus several years of experience working as reporters or editors for daily newspapers. Many of them have very successful careers in public relations. Undeniably, an understanding of the day-to-day operations of the print media and a feeling for the routine of the journalist are useful to a PIO. Nonetheless, public relations professionals differ from journalists in personality, motivation, training, and orientation.

Good reporters are distinguished by their intelligence, their curiosity and storytelling sense (their "nose for news"), their belief that they are engaged in an honorable profession, their skepticism, and their fondness for a lively argument. They are somewhat indifferent to money, since only the top people in the profession make high salaries. They tend to be independent and to value autonomy. They often work in solitude, spending a great deal of time gathering facts and writing.

Public relations professionals, in contrast, are oriented primarily toward business. In essence, they are salespeople, selling an image rather than a product. They choose public relations knowing that the field offers more substantial salaries and benefits than journalism does. They avoid the limelight, preferring to work behind the scenes, but they are capable of managing the public relations effort with a strong and steady hand. They are likely to be uncomfortable with the tensions and conflicts associated with investigative reporting, preferring the casual collegiality of the public relations office. They are not ideologues but are willing to embrace and espouse someone else's philosophy: the college president's.

This last point is important. Only one person can define the mission and goals of an organization, and that is the chief executive officer of that organization, whose primary duty it is to explain and interpret the role of the college to the community. An effective public information officer assists the CEO in performing this duty.

A corollary of the latter proposition is that the PIO must report directly or indirectly to the CEO and must over time develop a close working relationship with him or her. Only under such conditions can the PIO internalize the CEO's values, and only then can the CEO trust the PIO to communicate those values to the public. This process cannot be bypassed or shortcut. Some colleges may be flexible enough to allow the PIO to report to a dean, but—informally, at least—the PIO must have free and regular access to the CEO. Otherwise, the needed level of trust cannot be established.

In the absence of such access, the college's public relations effort is likely to be reactive, rather than proactive, and amount to little more than the churning out of press releases that describe campus events. An even greater risk is that the PIO will convey the wrong messages to the community.

## Organizing for Action

In mounting an effective public relations effort, the community college draws on a variety of resources. Any such effort must be coordinated with the college's overall marketing activities and must make optimal use of the public relations office staff.

*Coordination with Marketing Activities.* College marketing efforts are performed in a wide variety of settings by individuals with widely varying job titles. In many cases, the director of admissions, whose background is in counseling and student services, is expected to have marketing expertise. In other cases, the PIO is regarded as the in-house marketing expert. Some colleges, typically larger institutions, assign the marketing function to a specialist with a background in business and marketing. However organized, public relations must be viewed as an integral part of the college's total marketing effort. The PIO must work closely with whomever is in charge of the overall marketing effort and must be familiar with the long-range marketing plan in order to present a consistent vision of the college. Close coordination is of critical importance, since a college that sends out mixed messages to the community loses both credibility and public support.

The PIO must carefully review all brochures, advertisements, and other forms of communication to make sure that a clear and consistent message is being sent. If, for example, faculty and administrators have decided that the college's instructional future lies in industrial robotics and that its allied health programs should be phased out, then the college's brochures and viewbooks should not emphasize the strength and prestige of its allied health programs. Similarly, the PIO may conduct an impressive campaign—using mobile registration vans, booths at the county fair, balloons, and other hard-sell devices—to promote the college's image of homeyness and accessibility. He or she may even succeed in attracting large numbers of students through these efforts, but if the college's long-term plan calls for the development of its transfer function—with an emphasis on university-parallel programs, honors programs, and no-need scholarships—then this kind of promotional campaign is inappropriate and even counterproductive.

*The Public Relations Office.* An effective public relations program is a team effort, requiring at least three individuals: a director (the PIO), a writer, and an assistant/secretary. In addition to having significant managerial experience involving communications, the director should have writing and editing skills, since he or she is responsible for the quality of the office's output. As mentioned, the director should either report directly to the CEO or should meet with the CEO regularly to plan and implement the public relations strategy. The director is also responsible for making contact with the media and, at the request of the CEO, serves as the college's spokesperson.

With an experienced manager in place, the addition of a writer magnifies the office's effectiveness. A good writer should be able to produce about 5,000 words per week of news releases or similar material. The assistant/secretary is assigned such tasks as maintaining media contact lists, preparing releases and photos for distribution, maintaining such services as a speakers' bureau, editing the college's in-house newsletter, and keeping up with correspondence.

If possible, the college should provide each member of the public relations team with a networked personal computer or a word processor. The use of this technology greatly speeds the editing process and may significantly reduce typesetting costs. Moreover, the current trend is to distribute news releases computer to computer, thereby gaining immediacy and obviating the need to rekeyboard copy at the newspaper office.

*Relations with the Media.* The college president should implement a policy requiring that the media make initial contact with the college through the public relations office. While such a restriction may be misinterpreted, most faculty members and administrators will welcome it, since it serves to protect them from embarrassment and other unfortunate consequences of misstatement. After establishing a reporter's intent, the PIO may well recommend that a college employee talk with the reporter. This procedure also gives the PIO an opportunity to prepare the employee for the interview.

Needless to say, the PIO should maintain cordial and amicable relations with the various news media. In that way, the public relations office can take advantage of the many opportunities offered for free communications. The college will not have to devote any large portion of its fiscal resources to paid forms of advertising and promotion if it uses these available free channels to the fullest.

## The Public Relations Plan

As a first step in establishing an effective proactive public relations program, a comprehensive plan should be developed. It should address the following questions.

1. What long-term image does the college wish to project? What characteristics (low cost, accessibility, high-tech programs, high standards) does it want to emphasize?
2. What image does the college currently project?
3. How can the college's long-range plan be advanced through increased public understanding?
4. What are the specific goals of the public relations program?
5. What tactics should be used to achieve these goals?
6. How can the effectiveness of the public relations program be evaluated? What specific measures should be used?

The plan should be developed by a task force of senior-level administrators and faculty members. It should be reviewed and endorsed by the college president. Research must be undertaken to determine the college's current image in the community. Such research should employ quantitative methods (for example, opinion surveys) as well as qualitative techniques (for example, "focus group" panels).

Once approved, the plan should serve to guide the college's public relations effort over the long run. It should be reviewed annually, by means of a formal assessment of its effectiveness. Any decision to change its long-term strategic direction should be made only after the most careful consideration and deliberation. Building a college's public image takes time, and that image cannot be revised overnight.

## Proactive Public Relations in Practice

Public relations professionals are evaluated on their ability to attract coverage for events and ideas that otherwise would have been overlooked. Obviously, a certain amount of media manipulation is involved; just how much is a matter of ethical judgment. Recently, for example, a nationally televised beauty contest was reportedly almost cancelled at the last moment because the host, an animal-rights advocate, claimed that he would not appear if the contestants wore fur coats, as they were supposed to do in one of the events. The problem was resolved with the decision that they would wear fake fur instead. Meanwhile, the national news media gave the controversy (and the beauty pageant) several million dollars' worth of free coverage. On a radio talk show devoted to a debate on the issue of real versus artificial fur, one caller, who said he worked in public relations, labeled the entire incident a public relations gimmick. If so, it seems to have been effective, although most people would probably regard it as unethical, because it manufactured news. To the extent that it aroused widespread public suspicion about the host's motives and evoked a cynical response ("It's just a lot of hype"), this particular example must be viewed as unsuccessful. When practiced successfully, proactive public relations is difficult to spot, because it seems to appear naturally in the news environment.

An excellent example of proactive public relations comes from St. Petersburg Junior College, which offers what is calls the Alternative Learning Program, a remedial program for underprepared students. Such programs pose an image problem for many colleges. They fear the implication that some of their students are less than academically able. Therefore, they ignore these programs in their news releases or hide them under the euphemism *developmental education*. St. Petersburg, however, took a more positive approach, presenting its remedial program as a possible solution to some of the social problems described by current critics of American education. The Alternative Learning Program became the subject of a T.V. news feature, which treated it as a community service of the highest quality and merit. Colleges whose long-range plans call for projecting the image of a solver of social problems would do well to emulate this example.

Another example of proactive public relations is the handling of enrollment reports at the American Association of Community and Junior Colleges (AACJC). Knowing that the public is concerned over the high cost of college education and that such concern is likely to continue in the face of federal and state reductions in support, AACJC uses its news releases to link data on enrollment increases with information on low tuition in the community, technical, and junior college segments of postsecondary education. By making this link explicit, rather than waiting for the media to make the connection, AACJC is able to project an image of its member institutions as low-cost and accessible.

In summary, a proactive public relations program involves a deliberate effort to project a desired image of the college and thereby to change public attitudes and win community support for the college. By contrast, reactive public relations is characterized by an emphasis on events, without reference to any long-range set of objectives. Such efforts may result in media coverage, but they represent opportunities squandered.

*Daniel D. Savage is vice-president for communications services at the American Association of Community and Junior Colleges.*

*Educators who combine vision with ethics are ready to meet
the demands of the changing environment.*

# Summary and Conclusions

## Wellford W. Wilms, Richard W. Moore

World conditions can be likened to Chicago's weather: The only certainty
is that they will change. Spurred by demands for increased economic
productivity to maintain competitiveness in an unpredictable world
market, America's training and educational institutions have now begun
to respond. Although no one yet knows how new technologies, which
are designed to boost productivity, will affect employer demand, most
observers agree that changes are coming with increasing rapidity. Also,
older females and minorities will comprise an increasing share of the
typical community college and proprietary school, as more of them move
into the labor market. Although public community colleges are burdened
with incentives to resist change for the sake of stability, many are finding
it necessary to adopt agressive marketing techniques from proprietary
schools and business. Just how successful they will be in weathering the
turbulent times ahead remains an open question.

Duscha points to the increasing importance of job training in
fostering economic productivity and explores the potential of performance contracting to better link employers' demands for skilled labor
with supply. He notes that while most large employers prefer to do their
own training (although an increasing amount of it is being subsidized by
California's Employment Training Panel), community colleges and proprietary schools may have a unique niche in providing training for
medium-size and small firms. Duscha also describes the need in times of

W. W. Wilms and R. W. Moore (eds.). *Marketing Strategies for Changing Times.*
New Directions for Community Colleges, no. 60. San Francisco: Jossey-Bass, Winter 1987.

shrinking resources for cooperation across educational and training institutions to ensure that future workers are not only skilled but have solid educational backgrounds as well.

Thor describes how performance contracting works in the community college setting. While she is quick to point out its strong points (chiefly providing a new link with the world around the college, including employers), she also describes the risks publicly funded colleges run when they contract for training under California's Employment Training Panel or the federal Job Training Partnership Act. Of particular interest to community college administrators is Thor's description of specific steps that can be taken to manage that risk.

Similarly, Johnston's case study of a proprietary school gives other proprietary school owners and community college administrators new ways of linking their programs with the larger community. In particular, he pays close attention to ways his college forged links with local employers—an important means of quickly transmitting changes in the labor market to the school for inclusion in the curriculum.

Brannick, Boatright and Crowley, and Moore shift the discussion to what one converted community college administrator calls the three keys to survival in today's world—marketing, marketing, and more marketing! Brannick describes how his large corporation regards students as consumers with choices, a vision that ten years ago would have eluded most educators and offended the rest. Brannick writes globally about marketing yet gives the reader important insights into the nuts and bolts of moving educational products to the marketplace.

Boatright and Crowley show how marketing concepts were successfully used in the Houston Community College District to boost enrollments and connect the college more directly to changing labor conditions in the market.

Moore, in contrast, discusses how proprietary schools and community colleges have used market research tools to respond to market changes. He shows the school owner or administrator how to analyze the college's student clienteles—their demographics, media habits, shopping behavior, commuting patterns, and satisfaction with educational programs. Moore takes the reader through ways of gaining detailed knowledge about the student markets and uses U.S. Census data to penetrate them further.

Finally, Savage discusses the need for public relations to align market signals with public perceptions of the community college. In discussing the importance of market research to the community college, Savage shows specific steps administrators can take to build or strengthen their own public information offices.

In conclusion, as they search for reliable, trained workers, it is becoming increasingly clear that employers' expectations for training institutions have changed. Resource shortages have brought on demands for results. Similarly, as educational and training resources have shrunk, the state and federal governments have demanded that trainers do more with less. Thus, performance contracting has been embraced by the federal Job Training Partnership Act, as well as by the California Employment Training Panel. Preliminary results indicate that the California Employment Training Panel gets results. Without doubt, demands for economic productivity, which have become policy, require successful schools and colleges to form working links with employers to ensure that jobs lie at the end of training.

So far, the evidence points to the fact that some institutions have been able to adapt to this new environment quite well and to prosper, while others have not and are rapidly falling behind. What seems to make the difference is vision—of owners, managers, and administrators who are willing to look at the world in a new way and can see the impact of external events before they happen. When events do happen, successful school owners and administrators are ready, having put to work marketing and management techniques formerly reserved for the business world alone.

Although many educators have begun to accept the need for effective marketing techniques, care must be taken to ensure that demands for students do not overshadow ethical judgment. Particularly with respect to the provision of such human services as education and training, many students are drawn from the lower rungs of the socioeconomic ladder. To them, an investment of time and money represents a once-in-a-lifetime chance to become productive workers and citizens. Thus, it is incumbent upon educators to ensure that marketing is done within ethical limits and that the claims of advertising are substantiated.

*Wellford W. Wilms is associate professor and assistant dean of students in the Graduate School of Education at the University of Los Angeles.*

*Richard W. Moore is the executive director of Training Research Corporation.*

*This chapter offers an annotated bibliography of ERIC documents and articles.*

# Sources and Information: Reaching Employer and Student Markets

*Anita Y. Colby, Mary P. Hardy*

This chapter provides an annotated bibliography of recent ERIC documents and journal articles dealing with approaches taken by two-year colleges to assess and reach employer and student markets. The ERIC documents and journal articles in the bibliography were selected from additions to the ERIC database since 1980. *Marketing the Program,* New Directions for Community Colleges, no. 36, provides a review of ERIC materials published prior to that time.

The bibliography is presented in three sections. The first section looks at ways in which two-year colleges have assessed the educational needs and interests of their service areas, focusing on environmental scanning studies, community surveys, and employer needs assessments. The second section highlights descriptions of community college programs for local employers, including those funded under the Job Training Partnership Act. The final section includes both descriptions of and guidelines for the marketing efforts of community colleges and proprietary schools.

Unless otherwise indicated, the ERIC documents listed in this bibliography are available in microfiche or paper copy from the ERIC

W. W. Wilms and R. W. Moore (eds.). *Marketing Strategies for Changing Times.*
New Directions for Community Colleges, no. 60. San Francisco: Jossey-Bass, Winter 1987.

Document Reproduction Service (EDRS), 3900 Wheeler Ave., Alexandria, Va. 22304-5110 (1-800-227-3742). The microfiche price for documents under 481 pages is $0.78. Prices for paper copies are 1–25, $1.85; 25–50 pages, $3.70; for each additional 25 pages, add $1.85. These prices are subject to change. Postage must be added to all orders. The journal articles included in this bibliography are not available from EDRS and must be obtained through regular library channels.

**Needs Assessment**

Banerdt, J. *Needs Assessment for a Labor Studies Program in Cooperation with Gateway Technical Institute and the University of Wisconsin Parkside.* Kenosha, Wisc.: Gateway Technical Institute, 1980. 20 pp. (ED 192 859)
    Reports on a survey of the leaders of the 124 union locals in southeastern Wisconsin. The survey was conducted to identify the need for a structured, associate degree program in labor studies. The survey solicited information on membership size, the practice of hiring an education director, the types of educational programs that union members participate in, the willingness of local officials to serve on an advisory committee for the labor studies program, and the level of interest in such a program and in seventeen labor studies topics. Data tables and the questionnaire are included.

Benne, L. L. *Vocational Outreach Program.* Ottumwa, Iowa: Indian Hills Community College, 1984. 30 pp. (ED 246 966)
    Describes a manpower study conducted by Indian Hills Community College to gather local labor-market information, determine training needs, and assess the effectiveness of the college's vocational programs. Explains study methodology, which involved instructors from 20 vocational programs visiting and conducting interviews with 347 private and public sector employers.

Clagett, C. A. *ENSCAN 87: Environmental Scanning Report for Fiscal Year 1987.* Vol. 1: *The County.* Report PB87-1. Largo, Md.: Prince George's Community College, 1986. 49 pp. (ED 280 530)
    A result of a comprehensive environmental scan conducted by Prince George's Community College. This report reviews population trends and forecasts in Prince George's County, county and metropolitan area economic trends and forecasts, and college credit enrollment projections. Includes data displays covering national trends in workforce demographics, economic conditions, job outlook, changing age distribution, and educational consequences.

Clagett, C. A. *ENSCAN 87: Environmental Scanning Report for Fiscal Year 1987.* Vol. 2: *The College.* Report PB87-1. Largo, Md.: Prince George's Community College, 1986. 40 pp. (ED 280 531)

A second component of Prince George's Community College's comprehensive environmental scan. This report focuses on trends in the college's market share, student recruitment and retention, and enrollments. Includes data displays and findings from a statewide student retention study, providing information on 1980, 1981, and 1982 cohorts.

Cuyahoga Community College. *Planning for the 80s: Workforce Educational Development Project Report.* Cleveland, Ohio: Cuyahoga Community College, 1980. 94 pp. (ED 197 796)

Describes a needs assessment and a cooperative planning process used by Cuyahoga Community College to determine the best way of meeting the training and educational needs of the employed adults in its service district. Includes reports by apprenticeship, banking, health, insurance, and investment organizations; nonprofit agencies; and preretirement, public relations and communications, skills training in industry, and small-business task forces.

Engleberg, I. N., and Leach, E. R. (eds.). *Prince George's Community College Marketing Plan, 1981–1982.* Largo, Md.: Prince George's Community College, 1981. 178 pp. (ED 207 625)

Developed by the Marketing Task Force at Prince George's Community College in 1981. This report presents a plan that identifies educational service needs, recommends strategies for responding to those needs, and suggests a marketing approach. It ranks a total of ninety-six marketing tactics by priority under specific strategy categories, indicating the target market, office responsible, and planned completion date.

Glenn, H. W. *A Review of Present and Proposed Occupational and Degree Programs Offered by the Saddleback Community College District and the Labor Market in Orange County.* Mission Viejo, Calif.: Saddleback Community College District, 1985. 74 pp. (ED 265 896)

Designed to assist in determining the need for the present and proposed occupational and degree programs offered by Saddleback Community College District (SCCD). This report examines selected demographic and labor-market data related to industrial and occupational trends in Orange County, California, and employment opportunities for SCCD program graduates. It includes comparisons of SCCD's current occupational programs and certificate options with projected job openings in Orange County by 1990.

Griffin, D. J. *Survey Report of Occupational and Training Needs Within Service Delivery Area-1*. Blountville, Tenn.: Tri-Cities State Technical Institute, 1984. 133 pp. (ED 266 836)

Describes a comprehensive study of service and manufacturing industries within the five-county planning area of Tri-Cities Technical Institute, conducted in order to obtain information regarding employment and training needs and to increase awareness and utilization of the on-the-job training and targeted job tax credit programs available through the Job Training Partnership Act (JTPA). It includes on-site interview schedules, as well as samples of mailed questionnaires.

Johnson, B. E. *The DeKalb County Business-Industry-Labor-Student (BILS) Needs Assessment*. Clarkston, Ga.: DeKalb Area Vocational-Technical School, 1985. 74 pp. (ED 257 493)

Presents findings of a study conducted to investigate the educational and training needs of the community served by DeKalb Community College (DKCC) and DeKalb Area Technical School. It reports on results of interviews with 387 employers and in-class surveys of 512 part-time students, focusing on community awareness of DKCC and Dekalb Tech, the short-term educational/training needs of DeKalb employers and students, and the DKCC and DeKalb Tech units that would best fulfill the needs of employers and students. The survey instrument is included.

Klinman, D. G. *Employer Needs Assessment Project: Final Report*. Trenton, N.J.: Mercer County Community College, 1981. 75 pp. (ED 203 911)

Presents findings of a large-scale employer needs assessment, during which 1,140 Mercer County employers were contacted in order to assess employers' practices and preferences in recruitment of personnel; determine employer satisfaction with the college's ability to educate students for meaningful employment; analyze current and future manpower demands; assess employer needs and attitudes in relation to providing employees with additional skill training; and strengthen the college's relationship with the community by encouraging productive two-way communication. The survey instrument and an explanation of coding formats used for data analysis are included.

Kumar, V., and Tradewell, M.D.J. *Employer Needs Survey Report: A Report on Employer Needs and Thoughts about Programs, Courses, and Services*. Shell Lake, Wisc.: Indianhead Vocational, Technical, and Adult Education District, 1980. 171 pp. (ED 242 346)

Reports on an employer needs assessment conducted in the Wisconsin Indianhead Vocational, Technical, and Adult Education District to develop a profile of local employers' roles in training and determine employers' perceptions of Wisconsin Indianhead Technical Institute. The 33-item questionnaire is included.

Lyons, D. "Humboldt County Employer Survey." Prepared as part of the Humboldt County Labor Market Information Project and financed under the provisions of Title VII of the Comprehensive Employment and Training Act of 1973. Unpublished report, 1981. 139 pp. (ED 223 276)

Describes a project undertaken in Humboldt County, California, to collect information from 451 small and large businesses in the areas of agriculture, mining, manufacturing, transportation, wholesale and retail, finance, services, and public information, with respect to their requirements and needs for employees. Employer responses to open-ended questions, additional respondent comments, manufacturing firms' responses to economic questions, and the questionnaire are provided.

McCarty, L. *Transportation and Educational Needs of Industrial Airport Businesses.* Overland Park, Kans.: Johnson County Community College, 1980. 29 pp. (ED 215 715)

Presents the results of a survey conducted by Johnson County Community College to identify the education and transportation needs of Johnson County Industrial Airport employees and to determine employer educational requirements for employees and interest in courses. Information on company characteristics, employee education requirements, in-house training programs, subjects of interest, and preferred location for courses is included.

Marlette, J. M. *Facilitating Economic Development Through Linkages Between Vocational Education, CETA, and Small Businesses: Final Report.* Eau Claire, Wisc.: Wisconsin Vocational, Technical, and Adult Education District 1, 1981. 103 pp. (ED 220 168)

Describes a project undertaken by the Wisconsin Vocational, Technical, and Adult Education District 1 to determine the training and development needs of new small businesses and to establish vocational educational linkages between Comprehensive Employment and Training Act programs and these businesses. The project involved a survey of 915 business representatives, interviews with 525 small-business owners/ operators, conferences on resources to assist small businesses, and a video-tape presentation depicting the services available to businesses. Procedural recommendations and the survey instrument are included.

Mid-Florida Research and Business Center. *Excerpts from Daytona Beach Community College Institutional Audit.* Daytona Beach, Fla.: Daytona Beach Community College, 1985. 24 pp. (ED 269 060)

Presents the findings of a study that gathered information from county residents, educators, employers, and high school juniors and seniors to determine the market for the educational services that fall within the mission of Daytona Beach Community College, to identify target populations within that market, explore educational needs and perceived desires, and examine community opinions of the college and its academic services. Recommendations concerning marketing and institutional promotion are provided.

Moore, C. "An Assessment of the Attitudes and Program Needs of Commercial, Industrial, and Service Agencies from the Service Area of Worthington Community College." Unpublished Ed.D. dissertation, Nova University, 1980. 121 pp. (ED 198 889)

After providing a review of relevant literature, describes methodology and procedures, details findings, and presents summary recommendations for a study of 299 businesses representing a stratified random sample of service, commercial, and industrial employers in southwestern Minnesota. The study sought to determine the attitude of business executives toward Worthington Community College and to identify their postsecondary program needs. A bibliography, pilot-tested and final survey instruments, and a pilot study report are appended.

Muraski, E. J. *A Needs Assessment to Determine Employment Needs in Monroe County, Florida.* Key West, Fla.: Florida Keys Community College, 1982. 71 pp. (ED 223 272)

Describes a study conducted to determine the employment needs in Monroe County as the basis for planning and revising programs at Florida Keys Community College (FKCC). Surveys sent to a random sample of employers requested information on the firm; the importance of programs offered in Monroe County by high schools, adult and employment programs, and FKCC in relation to employers' needs; the current number of workers employed and their job categories; and projected changes in employers' needs over the next five years. The survey instrument is included.

Nasman, L. O. *A Model Package to Assess the Education and Training Needs of Business, Industry, and Labor.* Columbus, Ohio: National Postsecondary Alliance, 1981. 63 pp. (ED 237 139)

Designed for community colleges and technical institutes, this manual presents a systematic approach to the process of reviewing employer and employee education training needs utilizing the Business, Industry, and Labor Needs Assessment Model. It details sixteen procedures, delineates the responsibilities of the assessment team, and provides materials illustrating various data-gathering strategies. Included are background information related to the development of the model and a review of its pilot testing in Orangeburg, South Carolina; Dallas, Texas; and Wausau, Wisconsin.

Otis, L. L. *Vocational Learning Centers: A Link to Business and Industry.* Ashland: Wisconsin Indianhead Technical Institute, 1980. 16 pp. (ED 192 842)

Presents the findings of a survey of 100 businesses and industries in Ashland, Wisconsin, conducted to determine the perceived need for a shared informational media center to be used for workshops, training sessions, and in-service meetings. It describes the materials and facilities of Wisconsin Indianhead Technical Institute's Learning Resource Center that could be used in developing the shared center.

Poort, S. M., and Williamson, T. *Indian Hills Community College Vocational Outreach Program: Business/Industry and Indian Hills . . . Partners in Progress.* Ottumwa, Iowa: Indian Hills Community College, 1982. 32 pp. (ED 221 254)

Describes a study that utilized structured interviews to determine current and projected employment and training needs of private sector businesses with 200 or fewer employees and to assess opinions of Indian Hills Community College's programs. The survey instrument and study timetables are included.

Rosen, M. I., Schwab, D. P., Strang, W. A., and Nowrasteh, D. M. *Employment and Training Expectations of Employers in Area Vocational, Technical, and Adult Education District 4.* Madison, Wisc.: Madison Area Technical College, 1982. 102 pp. (ED 238 503)

Describes a study that sought to provide information on how Area Vocational Technical and Adult Education District 4 could more effectively serve the needs of area employers. It assesses potential growth or decline industries, occupations, and skill areas with implications for current and future vocational training programs and reports on the extent to which employers make use of District 4 graduates, as well as their views of graduates' work habits and occupational preparation. Survey instruments are included.

Saskatchewan Department of Advanced Education and Manpower. *Partners in Economic Growth: High Technology Industry and Postsecondary Education. The Report of the Task Force on High Technology.* Saskatoon, Saskatchewan, Canada: Saskatchewan Department of Advanced Education and Manpower, 1983. 38 pp. (ED 254 261)

Presents an analysis of the adequacy of Saskatchewan's technical institutes to satisfy the skilled labor needs of the emergent high-technology industry. The report offers recommendations and guiding principles for the development of the industry in the province and presents results of a survey of high-technology firms, indicating current industry characteristics, rates of growth and future needs, and high-technology employment growth. It outlines the educational requirements for entry-level employment and for continuing education and assesses current high-technology programs in Saskatchewan's technical institute system.

Stoehr, K. W., and Banerdt, J. *Walworth County Employer Needs Assessment Study*. Kenosha, Wisc.: Gateway Technical Institute, 1983. 43 pp. (ED 229 097)
    Presents an overview of a study conducted to assist Gateway Technical Institute (GTI) in providing programs and services to meet employers' manpower needs. The study's survey requested information from businesses, industries, and agencies in Walworth County concerning their characteristics, special high-technology training needs, plans for expansion, on-site provisions, interest in cooperative training programs with GTI, and evaluation of GTI-trained personnel. Survey results, recommendations, and the questionnaire are included.

University of Hawaii, Office of the Chancellor for Community Colleges. *Interreliance: An Energy Awareness Project for Community Colleges. A Report of the Task Force on Energy Education*. Honolulu, Hawaii: University of Hawaii, 1982. 51 pp. (ED 214 587)
    Describes the activities and recommendations of the Chancellor's Energy Task Force, which was established to give emphasis and direction to systemwide energy education efforts within the Hawaii community colleges. The document contains a local manpower and feasibility study report, which identifies alternative energy sources and considers findings in industry growth plans and potential, industry's labor needs over a five-year period, and requisite employee skills.

Young, D. A. *The Markets of the 1980s*. Canton, Ohio: Stark Technical College, 1980. 125 pp. (ED 190 174)
    Analyzes findings and provides resultant recommendations concerning future curriculum development at Stark Technical College (STC), based on surveys of selected employers (private businesses, government, healthcare institutions, professional services, and communications firms) and high school seniors from five high schools representing urban, suburban, rural, public, and private institutions. It discusses the occupational outlook of STC's service district on the basis of government, demographic, enrollment, and workforce data. The questionnaires and a bibliography are appended.

## Reaching Out to Employer Markets

American Association of Community and Junior Colleges. *Responding to the Challenge of a Changing American Economy: 1985 Progress Report on the Sears Partnership Development Fund.* Washington, D.C.: American Association of Community and Junior Colleges, 1986. 20 pp. (ED 270 144)

Describes the activities undertaken by the American Association of Community and Junior Colleges and the Association of Community College Trustees to enhance collaboration among community, technical, and junior colleges and business, industry, and labor; public employers; small businesses; and high schools. It highlights the awarding of twenty-nine partnership development minigrants to colleges; research and publication efforts; a collaborative project undertaken with the National Telecommunications Education Committee to help colleges develop curricula for the telecommunications industry; and program conferences and workshops.

Burger, L. T. "The Progress of Partners." *Community and Junior College Journal,* 1984, 55 (3), 36–39.

Looks at the Illinois community colleges' involvement in economic development through a network of business centers operated by all of the state's thirty-nine districts. It describes the programs and services offered by the colleges in such areas as customized job training, training for small businesses, contract procurement assistance, and Job Training Partnership Act involvement.

Duscha, S. "Retooling for Productivity." *Community and Junior College Journal,* 1984, 55 (3), 40–42.

Describes California's Employment Training Panel, which, with the assistance of progressive community colleges, has established unusual partnerships with businesses and workers to help foster job training and a more productive economy. The article looks at program qualifications and activities at the participating colleges.

Edge, B., and MacDonald, W. J. "Profitable Partnerships: Public-Private Partners in Economic Development." Paper presented at the third annual conference of the Council for the Advancement and Support of Education, Alexandria, Va., December 9–11, 1986. 45 pp. (ED 278 436)

Presents four case studies to demonstrate the economic development potential of partnerships between community colleges and public and private sectors, focusing on programs that targeted specific areas of need in Oregon's economic base and raised significant funds for program implementation. The paper includes detailed descriptions of Clatsop

Community College's Fisherman Technology Program; the Cascade Business Center Corporation, a business incubator operated by Portland Community College; the 2 + 2 + 2 Cooperative Honors Program in Electrical Engineering and Computer Engineering offered by Portland Community College, the University of Portland, and the Oregon Graduate Center; and EDNET, a statewide instructional television fixed-service microwave system developed by fifteen Oregon community colleges.

Fifield, M. L., and Sakamoto, C. M. (eds.). *The Next Challenge: Balancing International Competition and Cooperation*. Washington, D.C.: American Association for Community and Junior Colleges, 1987. 104 pp. (ED 280 548)
(Also available from AACJC Publications, 80 S. Early St., Alexandria Va. 22034; $9.40 for members, $12.50 for nonmembers)
     Presents sixteen essays addressing various aspects of the role of community colleges in international relations and trade. It offers descriptions of curriculum development efforts, community and information resources, sister-city projects, and consortial efforts to enable small community colleges to participate in international business education.

Jackman, M.J.G., and Mahoney, J. R. *Shoulders to the Wheel: Energy-Related College/Business Cooperative Agreements*. Washington, D.C.: American Association of Community and Junior Colleges, Energy Communications Center, 1982. 70 pp. (ED 214 584)
(Also available from AACJC Publications, 80 S. Early St., Alexandria, Va. 22034; $6.00)
     Provides information on cooperative agreements between college and industry, focusing special attention on such agreements in energy-related fields. The document offers a full case study of a cooperative agreement between Edmonds Community College and the Public Utility District Number 1 of Snohomish County, Washington, as well as brief descriptions of thirty-seven cooperative programs involving community colleges in twenty-one states. An analysis of cooperative agreements, some of their special features, and benefits and problems associated with their implementation are included.

Jellison, H. M. (ed.). *Small Business Training: A Guide for Program Building*. Washington, D.C.: American Association of Community and Junior Colleges, 1983. 68 pp. (ED 229 072)
(Also available from AACJC Publications, 80 S. Early St., Alexandria, Va. 22034; $10.00)
     Explains how community colleges can organize and deliver high-quality small-business training in a cost-effective manner. The document outlines steps for starting a small-business training program, describes

the types of programs offered by two-year institutions (credit programs, noncredit certificate programs, freestanding continuing education programs, alternative delivery systems, and special projects), and discusses such future directions as standardized training, contract education, and microcomputer instruction.

Jellison, H. M. (ed.). *Small Business Training Models for Community Growth.* Washington, D.C.: American Association of Community and Junior Colleges, 1983. 66 pp. (ED 229 062)
(Also available from AACJC Publications, 80 S. Early St., Alexandria, Va. 22034; $10.00)

Describes nine successful community college programs for small-business management training, focusing on college and economic contexts, purpose, offerings, delivery modes, operating and marketing strategies, community outreach, support services, faculty and staff, evaluation, and future directions. It includes descriptions of programs involving individual assistance to businesses, workshops, full degree programs, on-site consultation services, business conferences, and skills training.

Linthicum, D. S. *Economic Development Through Education at Maryland's Community Colleges.* Annapolis: Maryland State Board for Community Colleges, 1985. 73 pp. (ED 259 803)

Describes a study conducted to identify the role community colleges have played in developing Maryland's economic resources. The study methodology included a college survey requesting information on courses, programs, economic development activities, and relations with community businesses and agencies; interviews with personnel from eight community colleges; and a literature review and follow-up contacts to assess activities in other states. The survey instrument is included.

Ludwig, T., Crist, D. G., and Shoup, B. *Admiral Corporation and Carl Sandburg Community College Score Through JTPA.* Galesburg, Ill.: Carl Sandburg Community College, 1984. 7 pp. (ED 243 536)

Describes a joint project involving the Admiral Corporation, the Illinois Department of Commerce and Community Affairs, the Illinois State Board of Education, the Job Training Partnership Act, and Carl Sandburg Community College, in their effort to provide training and jobs for unemployed workers in Galesburg, Illinois. Steps taken in the joint project, which resulted in the training and employment of 138 workers, are explained.

Mahoney, J. R. *Community College Centers for Contracted Programs: A Sequel to Shoulders to the Wheel.* Washington, D.C.: American Associa-

tion of Community and Junior Colleges, 1982. 77 pp. (ED 229 061)
(Also available from AACJC Publications, 80 S. Early St., Alexandria,
Va. 22034; $6.00)

Provides a summary of the characteristics of special community
college centers that contract educational services to business, industry,
government, and other groups in the local community. The document
outlines factors that have influenced the creation of college and community centers and offers a composite profile of the centers' goals, objectives,
services, contact and linkage approaches, program development procedures, and administrative details. It discusses problems experienced by
existing centers and offers advice on initiating or expanding involvement
in contracted educational services. Brief case studies of centers at fifteen
colleges are included.

Mahoney, J. R., and Sakamoto, C. (eds.). *International Trade and Educa-*
*tion: Issues and Programs.* AACJC Issues Series, no. 2. Washington,
D.C.: American Association of Community and Junior Colleges, 1985.
90 pp. (ED 261 723)
(Also available from AACJC Publications, 80 S. Early St., Alexandria,
Va. 22034; $10.00)

Contains seventeen articles designed to give college officials
insights into international trade education programs and services offered
by a number of postsecondary institutions; to identify problems experienced by program administrators; and to share the perspectives of leaders
in international trade education. The articles consider such aspects of
international trade education as intercultural training, cultural awareness
training, foreign language needs, research needs, business and education
cooperation, and faculty upgrading.

**The Use of Marketing Techniques in Public Relations,**
**Student Recruitment, and Image Enhancement**

Ash, B. F. "Marketing Continuing Education Programs in the Public-
Supported Community College." Paper presented to Phi Delta Kappa,
Boston University, 1986. 27 pp. (ED 270 143)

Describes the marketing philosophy and strategies of Bunker Hill
Community College. The paper highlights the following participant motivation and marketing strategies: working with business and industry to
provide skill upgrading and retraining for blue-collar workers; teaching
in a variety of instructional modes designed to match the learning styles
of older adults and students of lower socioeconomic status; involving
adult students in the planning, organization, and implementation of the
curriculum; utilizing personal contacts as a means of disseminating information on programs to low-income workers; and utilizing media for

recruitment of white-collar workers. The college's mathematical model for arriving at fees for its continuing education offerings is presented.

Blanchard, B. *Applying Marketing Concepts to Higher Education: Development of an Enrollment Management Plan for the Off-Campus Program.* Warwick: Community College of Rhode Island, 1985. 78 pp. (ED 271 151)

Provides a comprehensive enrollment management plan for the Off-Campus Program offered by the Community College of Rhode Island. The document offers specific recommendations for institutional research needs, the creation of advisory boards, the development of flexible course schedules, the provision of incentive and recognition awards, the expansion of the high school enrichment program and business/industry linkages, and the improvement of television services. It also looks at ways to improve off-campus student services and methods of promoting the program and recruiting students.

Bogart, Q. J. "Four Structures for Marketing in the American Public Community College." Paper presented at the 64th annual national convention of the American Association of Community and Junior Colleges, Washington, D.C., April 1-4, 1984. 24 pp. (ED 253 279)

Examines the distinctive marketing practices of four geographically separated, public community college districts: California's Coastline Community College's central administration–dominated structure; Missouri's Metropolitan Community College District's marketing committee–dominated structure; Illinois's Triton College's marketing division–dominated structure; and Prince George's Community College's student services–dominated structure. The paper describes and assesses the main advantages and disadvantages of each structure.

Burdick, R. "Streamlining Student Search Materials: Developing a Plan." Paper presented at the third annual conference of the Council for the Advancement and Support of Education, Alexandria, Va., December 9-11, 1986. 23 pp. (ED 278 439)

Offers an overview of the factors to be considered in assessing and improving the quality and effectiveness of a college's recruitment materials. The paper compares various methods of conducting studies of students' perceptions of college publications and looks at the steps involved in creating and implementing a publications plan, including recommendations on the use of consultants and a discussion of cost considerations.

Desiderio, J. *Bringing Recruitment On-Line.* Scottville, Mich.: West Shore Community College, 1985. 15 pp. (ED 255 252)

Describes West Shore Community College's Prospective Student Contact System (PSCS), an on-line recruitment and student information system that provides a systematic process of communicating with prospective students, the mechanism and data to measure the effectiveness of recruitment efforts, a database of information on the curricular interests and demographic characteristics of applicants and prospective students, and information indicating which member of the college community has made contact with a prospective student, when, and where. Information on the computer configuration used to operate the PSCS is included.

Donsky, A. P., Karian, C., and Weeks, A. *Impact Measures for a Marketing Intervention Strategy at a Two-Year College.* Poughkeepsie, N.Y.: Dutchess Community College, 1986. 20 pp. (ED 272 242)

Describes and assesses the effectiveness of a marketing strategy implemented by Dutchess Community College in the summer of 1985. The project involved sending personalized letters to students who had been attending college elsewhere, encouraging them to enroll at their low-cost neighborhood community college during the upcoming summer and transfer the course credits back to their present institutions. A review of the literature on educational marketing is included.

Fonte, R., and Leach, E. (eds.). *Triton College Marketing Plan 1985–1986.* River Grove, Ill.: Triton College, 1985. 65 pp. (ED 263 931)

Provides an in-depth analysis of environmental conditions faced by Triton College and a specific marketing plan developed in response to the identified trends. The document focuses on trends related to general enrollment patterns, shifts within program categories, changes within the high school graduate pool, age shifts, minority student population growth, and occupational trends. Using detailed program objectives as a base, it presents specific plans for reaching new markets, developing or changing services and products, and improving institutional image.

Gehrung, F., Johnson, J., Petrizzo, D. R., and Stubler, M. "How Can Community Colleges Work with the Media to Improve Their Public Image?" *Community, Junior, and Technical College Journal,* 1986, *57* (1), 32–35.

Essays by four public relations specialists discuss how community colleges can increase their coverage in the media and improve their public image. The article considers reasons community colleges may not have received media coverage in the past and suggests ways in which institutions can improve their relations with the press and bring newsworthy stories to the media's attention.

Hamilton, J., and Hartstein, R. "Media and the Trustee." In G. F. Petty (ed.), *Active Trusteeship for a Changing Era.* New Directions for Community Colleges, no. 51. San Francisco: Jossey-Bass, 1985.

Underscores the importance of community college trustees' working effectively with the news media. The article discusses ways of protecting the institution's image, variables affecting image, public relations policies, the role of the board chair, marketing responsibilities, and trustee actions that can strain media relations. Offers guidelines for dealing with the media.

Kleinman, A. "Marketing and Sales for Proprietary Schools." *Career Training,* 1986, *2* (4), 8–11.

Provides several tips for marketing a proprietary school. The article offers suggestions related to newspaper and television advertising, direct mail, high school marketing, and the timing of promotional mailings.

Osborn, F. P. *Recap of Marketing Information Available to Monroe Community College, 1984–1985.* Rochester, N.Y.: Monroe Community College, 1985. 12 pp. (ED 269 063)

Provides an overview of the perceptions of the major constituencies of Monroe Community College about the college and of the internal and external marketing strategies being considered to promote the institution. The document presents research findings concerning the way the college is viewed by the community, faculty, and students. It discusses marketing and promotion issues in relation to the image the college wishes to project and identifies the information that should be disseminated to parents, high school students, adult women, the student body, faculty and staff, and student leaders.

Piland, W. E. "Beyond Needs Assessments: Marketing as Change Agent." *Community/Junior College Quarterly of Research and Practice,* 1984, *8* (1–4), 93–102.

Views marketing techniques as agents of change that can provide valuable assistance to community college decision makers. The article discusses the importance of a balance among the four $p$'s of marketing—promotion, price, place, and product—and outlines seven procedural steps in developing a sound marketing strategy.

Pitt Community College. *A Model for Recruiting the New Community College Student.* Greenville, N.C.: Pitt Community College, 1985. 159 pp. (ED 267 187)

Offers a proposal for revitalizing traditional recruitment practices and for establishing a new recruitment model for attracting the nontraditional student to North Carolina's two-year colleges. The document presents recommendations concerning internal and external population mapping; targeting such populations as senior citizens, occupationally mobile individuals, displaced homemakers, and dislocated workers; utilizing a market assessment index; and developing a marketing plan.

Silberg, C. A. *What Is the Relationship between the Effectiveness of Nonprofit Organizations' Marketing Techniques and Type of Audience Approached?* Largo, Md.: Prince George's Community College, 1984. 56 pp. (ED 254 287)

Reports on the methods and findings of a study conducted at Prince George's Community College (PGCC) to determine which marketing techniques used by the college were most effective in student recruitment, and whether the ways in which students heard about the college were related to the reasons they came to PGCC and their selections of majors. The report indicates that high school teachers had a greater than expected influence on transfer students, while mailed publications were less effective for transfer students and more effective than anticipated for students attending college to prepare for new careers or for self-enrichment. A literature review on marketing for nonprofit organizations is included.

Tatro, J. O. "Recruiting and Retaining Students from the Corporate Sector." *Community Services Catalyst,* 1986, *16* (1), 8-13.

Sees the corporate sector as a major potential market for colleges while warning of difficulties in recruiting and retaining corporate students. The author recommends that educators analyze the nature of their markets, determine what they are marketing, assess the degree to which administrative systems and policies support retention, and develop activities for strengthening support systems for corporate students.

Waltz, F. C., Arrington, L. R., Cheek, J. G., and Deeman, C. E. *A Recruitment Package for Postsecondary Vocational Education. From August 1, 1983 to August 31, 1984. Final Report.* Gainesville: Institute of Food and Agricultural Sciences, University of Florida, 1984. 145 pp. (ED 247 450)

Offers seven instructional units and a how-to guide to assist in the establishment and implementation of a recruitment program for postsecondary vocational education programs. The units focus on such topics as the nature of and rationale for recruitment; marketing; recruitment activities; the role of career information and counseling in recruitment; and evaluation methods. The guide deals with such aspects of recruitment as conducting a needs assessment; preparing marketing materials; writing advertising copy; planning a career awareness program; and developing a public relations proposal outline. Samples of recruitment materials are appended.

Warfield, D. *Florida Keys Community College's College Reach-Out Program.* Key West, Fla.: Florida Keys Community College, 1985. 24 pp. (ED 272 259)

Describes Florida Keys Community College's efforts to recruit black high school students through such programs as its Eighth Grade Visitation Program, High School Recruitment Program, Financial Aid Awareness Seminar, and College Visitation Day. A summary of the 1984–1985 activities of the College Reach-Out Program is provided.

Wilhelmi, C., Bradley, J. L., Burke, K. S., Grizzard, E. S., Miginnis, W., Mustachio, J., Palumbo, L. L., Rossmeier, J. G., and Witter, R. M. *Marketing Plan 1983–1984.* Annandale: Northern Virginia Community College, 1983. 86 pp. (ED 234 839)

Presents Northern Virginia Community College's 1983–1984 marketing plan, which was designed to maximize the effective use of shrinking resources to meet the needs of the college's clientele. The authors offer information on the development of the marketing plan and guidelines for twenty-eight specific marketing activities, which indicate the target audience for the marketing activity, strategies and tactics, evaluation criteria, and cost estimates.

Wilms, W. W. "Proprietary Schools: Strangers in Their Own Land." *Change,* 1987, *19* (1), 10–22.

Looks at the growing role played by proprietary schools in American postsecondary education. The article considers key factors that set them apart from traditional colleges and universities, focusing on aggressive marketing and advertising techniques, responsiveness to student and employer markets, and such characteristics as size, facilities, staffing, admissions, and teachers. The author profiles several proprietary school owners and examines recent court cases regarding misleading advertising and related licensing and regulation issues.

*Anita Y. Colby is associate director of the ERIC Clearinghouse for Junior Colleges, University of California, Los Angeles.*

*Mary P. Hardy is user services specialist at the ERIC Clearinghouse for Junior Colleges, University of California, Los Angeles.*

# Index

**A**

Admiral Corporation, 97
Advertising: brochures, 36; direct-mail, 65; newsletters, 56, 79; news-papers, 28, 56; television, 46
Advisory boards, 39, 99
Alternative Learning Program, at St. Petersburg Junior College, 81
American Association of Community and Junior Colleges (AACJC), 53, 81, 95–99
American Society of Training and Development, 57
Arrington, L. R., 102
Ash, B. F., 98–99
Assembly Office of Research (California), 9
Association of Community College Trustees, 53, 95

**B**

Bakersfield Innkeepers Association, 40
Banerdt, J., 88, 94
Basic literacy skills, 16, 21
BB College, market research study at, 70–71
Beder, H., 27–28, 32
Benne, L. L., 88
Better Business Bureau, 54
Bibliography: of market research in education, 72; of student and employer markets, 87–103
Blacks, 67, 71, 103; and training resources, 8; and vocational education, 12
Blanchard, B., 99
Blue-collar workers, retraining for, 98
Bluestone, B., 7, 13
Boatright, J., 54–55, 84
Bogart, Q. J., 99
Bolton, A., 9, 13
Boyle, P. G., 52, 59
Bradley, J. L., 103

Branch campuses, 48, 57, 67–68
Brannick, M. K., 11, 84
Brazil, 21
Bunker Hill Community College, 98–99
Burdick, R., 99
Bureau of Labor Statistics, 17, 21
Burger, L. T., 95
Burke, K. S., 103
Business, Industry, and Labor Needs Assessment Model, 92–93
Business-Industry-Community College Trustees Coalition, 53

**C**

Calder, B. J., 70, 72
California: community colleges and performance contracts, 25; public school enrollments in, 61
California Commission on Industrial Innovations, 12, 13
California Employment Development Department, 9, 13
Carl Sandburg Community College, 97
Cascade Business Center Corporation, 96
Cheek, J. G., 102
Chief executive officer (CEO), and effective public relations, 76
City Junior College, study of future enrollments at, 68–69
Civil Aeronautics Board, 11
Civil rights movement, 8
Clagett, C. A., 88–89
Clatsop Community College's Fisherman Technology Program, 95–96
Coastline Community College (California), 99
Community College of Rhode Island, 99
Community colleges, 6; and competition for students, 62; faculty of, 12; financing of, 8–9; and geographical markets, 64–65; and local political

Community Colleges *(continued)* processes, 12; market research studies at, 71; marketing practices of, 99; as nonmarket-oriented institutions, 12; and performance contracts, 23–25; and the public and private sector, 95–96; and public relations, 75–81; and small-business management training, 96–97; and student markets, 68–69

Community networks, establishing, 27

Company-specific programs, 57

Comprehensive Employment and Training Act, 91

Computers, 41, 48, 97, 100

Congress, and performance contracts, 24

Constantine, K. K., 72

Consumer research, 48

Contractors. *See* Performance contracts

Cooperative Institutuional Research Program's (CIRP) Freshman Survey, 64

Corporate classrooms, 15, 17, 20

Cost benefits, of market-driven organizations, 48

Cost-effectiveness, of marketing efforts, 45, 96–97

Council for the Advancement and Support of Education (Virginia), 95, 96, 99

Council on Postsecondary Education, 42

Crist, D. G., 97

Crowley, J., 84

Culley, J. D., 45, 50

Customer-oriented planning, 48–49, 50

Cuyahoga Community College, 89

**D**

Daytona Beach Community College, 91–92

Deeman, C. E., 102

DeKalb Area Technical School, 90

DeKalb Community College (DKCC), 90

Demographics: changing, 46, 61, 71–72; student, 64; variable, 65; workforce, 88

Desiderio, J., 99–100

Donnely Marketing, 65

Donsky, A. P., 100

Downs, A., 11, 13

Drucker, P. F., 5, 13

Duscha, S., 83–84, 95

Dutchess Community College (New York), 100

**E**

Economics, changes in world, 5–6, 21, 83

Edge, B., 95–96

Edmonds Community College, 96

EDNET, 96

Education: based on consumer demand, 8, 9; bibliography of market research in, 72; contract, 97; and ethics, 83–85; in international trade, 98; as a product, 43; selling, 46–47

Employer markets, documents and articles on, 87–103

Employers: as contractors of training, 31; and corporate classrooms, 20; and demographics, 6–8; input into training curriculum of, 29; needs assessment of, 90, 92–93; and retraining for employees, 19; and training for new workers, 19

Employment Training Panel (ETP), 10, 15–21, 24, 31, 83–85, 95; contracting history of, 18, 19; financial outcome of contracts with, 26

Employment training programs: advantages of, 31; budgeting for, 30; characteristics of successful, 29; described, 23–24

Employment-based contracts, 18

Endo, J. J., 72

Energy Communications Center of American Association of Community and Junior Colleges, 96

Engleberg, I. N., 89

Enrollments: increasing, through marketing, 41–50; projections, 88

ERIC, 87–88

Ethics: in education, 83–85; in marketing, 103

Eurich, N. P., 20, 21

Evaluation, 29; of job training in California, 16

Executive Service Directory (Houston), 54

**F**

Fifield, M. L., 96
Florida Keys Community College (FKCC), 92, 103
Fonte, R., 100
Four-year colleges, 17, 63; and marketing, 47; and prepayment of tuition, 47; and student enrollment, 69
Fox, K. F., 72

**G**

Gainesville Institute of Food and Agricultural Sciences, 102
Galleria Arts Center (Houston), 57
Gateway Technical Institute (GTI) (Wisconsin), 94
Gays, and training resources, 8
Gehrung, F., 100
Gelb Consulting Group, Inc., 54
General Electric, 7
Goldgehn, L. A., 53–54, 59
Gonzales, J., 27, 28, 32
Griffin, D. J., 90
Grizzard, E. S., 103
Grubb, N., 12, 13
Gulf Coast Consortium, 53–54, 58

**H**

Hamilton, J., 101
Hartstein, R., 101
High technology industry: needs assessment of, in Wisconsin, 94; needs assessment of, in Saskatchewan, 93
Hispanics, 46, 67, 76; and training resources, 8; and vocational education, 12
Homosexuals. See Gays, Lesbians
Houle, C. O., 52, 59
Houston Chamber of Commerce, 56–57
Houston Committee for Private Sector Initiatives, 57
Houston Community College System (HCCS), 51–59, 84
Houston Economic Council, 57

Houston Federation of Professional Women, 57
Houston Personnel Association, 57
Humboldt County Labor Market Information Project, 91

**I**

Illinois, business centers in, 95
Illinois Department of Commerce and Community Affairs, 97
Illinois State Board of Education, 97
Image enhancement, marketing techniques in, 98–103
India, 21
Indian Hills Community College, 88, 93
Indianhead Vocational, Technical, and Adult Education District, 90–91
In-house training programs, 56, 91
Internal Revenue Service, 11
International and Domestic Business Committee (Houston), 57
International relations, essays on the role of community colleges in, 96

**J**

Jackman, M.J.G., 54, 59, 96
Jassaud, D., 12, 13
Jellison, H. M., 96–97
Job training. See Employment training
Job Training Partnership Act (JTPA), 8, 9, 10, 24, 84, 85, 90, 95, 97; financial outcome of contracts with, 26; and performance-driven contracts with local SDAs, 24
Johnson, B. E., 90
Johnson County Community College, 91
Johnson County Industrial Airport, needs assessment of employees at, 91
Johnson, J., 100
Johnston, D., 11, 84
Jones, J., 55

**K**

Kane, E. J., 44, 50
Kaplan, D., 27–28, 32

Karian, C., 100
Kelley, E. J., 44, 50
Kleinman, A., 101
Klinman, D. G., 90
Knowles, M. S., 52, 59
Koltai, L., 13
Kotler, P., 53-54, 59, 72
Krafcik, J., 7, 13
Kumar, V., 90-91

**L**

Labor: changing demographics in, 6-8; and corporate training classrooms, 20; markets, 28, 89, 91; studies, 88
Lapin, J. D., 27, 32
Lay, R. S., 72
Lazer, W., 45, 50
Leach, E., 89, 100
Lesbians, and training resources, 8
Levin, H., 7, 13
Levitan, S., 7, 13
Levitt, T., 43, 50
Linthicum, D. S., 97
Long, C., 29, 32
Low-income students, 65
Ludwig, T., 97
Lynton, E., 6, 13
Lyons, D., 91

**M**

McCarty, L., 91
MacDonald, W. J., 95-96
McGarrity, R. A., 52, 59
Madison Area Technical College, 93
Mahoney, J. R., 54, 59, 96, 97-98
Market research: and changing demographics, 61-62; in education, 72; and student recruitment, 61-73; and studies of student markets, 67-72; tools, 84
Market Survey, by Houston Community College System, 54-55
Marketing: consultants at community colleges, 13; coordinating activities in, 78-79; importance of planning in, 48-49; increasing enrollments through, 41, 42-50; information systems, 47; and public relations, 75-81

Marketing Task Force, at Prince George's Community College, 89
Marketing-mix theory, 45-49
Markets: changes in world, 5, 6; documents and articles on employer, 95-98; geographical, 64-65; labor, 91; measuring, 66; orienting training institutions to, 10; predicting, 65, 67-68; reaching student and employer, 87-103; understanding, 69
Marlette, J. M., 91
Maryland State Board for Community Colleges, 97
Media, 44, 79, 98, 99-101; manipulation of, 80-81; use of, in recruitment, 99
Mercer Community College, 90
Metropolitan Community College District (Missouri), 99
Mexico, 21
Middle-class students, 65
Mid-Florida Research and Business Center, 91-92
Miginnis, W., 103
Military, and student recruitment, 62, 69
Minorities, 46, 61, 65, 83, 100
Monroe Community College (New York), 101
Moore, C., 92
Moore, R. W., 84
MR College, market research study at, 71
Muraski, E. J., 92
Murphy, P. E., 52, 59
Mustachio, J., 103

**N**

Nasman, L. O., 92-93
National Alliance of Business, 24, 32
National Decision Systems, 65
National Postsecondary Alliance, 92-93
National Telecommunications Education Committee, 95
Native Americans, and training resources, 8
Needs assessment, documents and articles concerning, 88-94
Networks, 56-58, 95

*Newsweek*, 52
Nisenfeld, L., 27, 28, 32
Northern Virginia Community College, 103
Nova University, 92
Nowrasteh, D. M., 93
Nye, G., 28, 29, 32

**O**

Occupational training, through Houston Community College System (HCCS), 52
Occupational trends, 100
Office of Business-Industry Development (Houston), 58
Oregon, economic case studies in, 95–96
Oregon Graduate Center, 96
Osborn, F. P., 101
Otis, L. L., 93

**P**

Palumbo, L. L., 103
Performance contracts, 9–12, 23–32, 83–85; defined, 9–10; employment-based, 18; financial management of, 30; the future of, 31–32; in Georgia, 9; in Ontario, Canada, 9; risk management in, 23–24; and state-funded employment training programs, 24
Perkins Vocational Education Act, 8
Personnel Policies Forum of the Bureau of National Affairs, 17, 18, 21
Petrizzo, D. R., 100
Piland, W. E., 101
Pitt Community College (North Carolina), 101–102
Placement director, 34–38
Planning: cooperative, 89; marketing strategy, 48–49; model for employment training programs, 28–31; and public relations, 80
Poort, S. M., 93
Portland Community College, 96
Postsecondary education: as an industry, 46; and the marketing concept, 42–50; and product strategy, 44
Prince George's Community College, 88, 89, 99, 102

Proprietary Market Information System (ProMIS), 64
Proprietary schools, 10–12, 75, 84; and the changing environment, 83–85; and competition for students, 62; and customer-directed education, 43; dependence on student tuitions at, 12–13; and geographical markets, 64–65; as heterogeneous institutions, 11; and local employers, 33–40; market research studies at, 70–71; marketing at, 101; and public relations, 75–81; and student markets, 67–68
Public Information Officer (PIO), and effective public relations, 77–80
Public institutions, and federal funding, 8
Public relations, 84, 89; and chief executive officers, 76–78; and ethics, 80–81; and marketing, 75–81, 98–103; and the media, 79; and planning, 80; proactive, 78–81; and Public Information Officers, 77–78
"Put America Back to Work" project, 53

**R**

Retraining: for blue-collar workers, 98; for existing employees, 19
Rose, C., 28–29, 32
Rosen, M. L., 93
Rossmeier, J. G., 103
Rumberger, R., 7, 13

**S**

Saddleback Community College District (SCCD), 89
St. Petersburg Junior College, 81
Sakamoto, C., 96, 98
Santa Barbara Business College (SBBC), 33–40; employer network at, 35; placement process at, 37–38; recruitment devices at, 38–39
Saskatchewan Department of Advanced Education and Manpower, 93–94
Saudi Arabia, 21
Savage, D. D., 84
Schwab, D. P., 93

Seminars, 36, 44, 46; company-specific, 56; professional development, 53, 54, 55
Service delivery areas (SDAs), 24
Shoup, B., 97
Silberg, C. A., 102
Skills training, 17, 89, 97, 98
Small businesses, 89, 91, 96, 97
Stark Technical College (STC), 94
State legislatures, and performance contracts, 24
State-funded employment training programs, and performance contracts, 24
Stoehr, K. W., 94
Strang, W. A., 93
Stubler, M., 100
Student markets: studies of, 67-72; sources and information on reaching, 87-103
Student recruitment, 70, 89; marketing techniques in, 98-103; through market research, 61-73
Students: as consumers, 62, 63-64; as customers, 42-45; and demographic changes, 6

**T**

Tatro, J. O., 102
Telemarketing, 36
Telephone surveys, 54, 55, 57
Testimonials: example of, 38; from employers, 38; from graduates, 38
Texas, public school enrollments in, 61
Thor, L. M., 25, 27, 31, 32, 84
Topor, R., 72
Tradewell, M.D.J., 90-91
Tri-Cities Technical Institute, 90
Triton College (Illinois), 99-100
Tuition: preannouncing future price increases in, 47; prepayment of, 47; reimbursement by employers, 58

**U**

Unemployed workers, training and jobs for, 97
Unions, study of, in Wisconsin, 88

U.S. Bureau of the Census, 6, 14, 65, 67-68, 84
U.S. Bureau of Labor Statistics, 7, 14
University extensions, 62
University of Hawaii, Office of the Chancellor for Community Colleges, 94
UR Business College, study of future enrollments at, 67, 68

**V**

Vocational Education Act, 30
Vocational training programs, needs assessment of, 93

**W**

Waltz, F. C., 102
Warfield, D., 103
Weeks, A., 100
Welfare, and performance contracts, 24
West Shore Community College (Michigan), 99-100
White-collar workers, recruitment of, 99
Wilhelmi, C., 103
Williamson, T., 93
Wilms, W. W., 7, 11, 14, 16, 21, 103
Wisconsin, survey of union locals in, 88
Wisconsin Indianhead Technical Institute, Labor Resource Center at, 93
Wisconsin Vocational, Technical, and Adult Education District, 91
Witter, R. M., 103
Womack, J., 7, 13
Women, 46, 83; and training resources, 8; and vocational education, 12
Worthington Community College, 92

**Y**

Young, D. A., 94

**Z**

Zip codes, as a market research tool, 65-68

US POSTAL SERVICE

## STATEMENT OF OWNERSHIP, MANAGEMENT AND CIRCULATION
(Required by 39 U.S.C. 3685)

| 1. TITLE OF PUBLICATION | | A. PUBLICATION NO. | | | | | | | 3. DATE OF FILING |
|---|---|---|---|---|---|---|---|---|---|
| New Directions for Community Colleges | | 1 | 2 | 1 | - | 7 | 1 | 0 | 10/7/87 |

| 2. FREQUENCY OF ISSUE | A. NO. OF ISSUES PUBLISHED ANNUALLY | B. ANNUAL SUBSCRIPTION PRICE |
|---|---|---|
| quarterly | 4 | $39 indiv/$52 inst |

4. COMPLETE MAILING ADDRESS OF KNOWN OFFICE OF PUBLICATION (Street, City, County, State and ZIP Code) (Not printers)

433 California St., San Francisco, San Francisco county, CA 94104

5. COMPLETE MAILING ADDRESS OF THE HEADQUARTERS OR GENERAL BUSINESS OFFICES OF THE PUBLISHERS (Not printers)

433 California St., San Francisco, San Francisco county, CA 94104

6. FULL NAMES AND COMPLETE MAILING ADDRESS OF PUBLISHER, EDITOR, AND MANAGING EDITOR (This item MUST NOT be blank)

PUBLISHER (Name and Complete Mailing Address)

Jossey-Bass Inc., Publishers, 433 California St., San Francisco CA 94104

EDITOR (Name and Complete Mailing Address)

Arthur Cohen, ERIC, 8118 Math Sciences Bldg., UCLA, Los Angeles CA 90024

MANAGING EDITOR (Name and Complete Mailing Address)

Allen Jossey-Bass, Jossey-Bass Publishers, 433 California St., SF CA 94104

7. OWNER (If owned by a corporation, its name and address must be stated and also immediately thereunder the names and addresses of stockholders owning or holding 1 percent or more of total amount of stock. If not owned by a corporation, the names and addresses of the individual owners must be given. If owned by a partnership or other unincorporated firm, its name and address, as well as that of each individual must be given. If the publication is published by a nonprofit organization, its name and address must be stated.) (Item must be completed.)

| FULL NAME | COMPLETE MAILING ADDRESS |
|---|---|
| Jossey-Bass Inc., Publishers | 433 California St., SF CA 94104 |

for names and addresses of stockholders, see attached list

8. KNOWN BONDHOLDERS, MORTGAGEES, AND OTHER SECURITY HOLDERS OWNING OR HOLDING 1 PERCENT OR MORE OF TOTAL AMOUNT OF BONDS, MORTGAGES OR OTHER SECURITIES (If there are none, so state)

| FULL NAME | COMPLETE MAILING ADDRESS |
|---|---|
| same as #7 | |

9. FOR COMPLETION BY NONPROFIT ORGANIZATIONS AUTHORIZED TO MAIL AT SPECIAL RATES (Section 411.3 DMM only)
The purpose, function, and nonprofit status of this organization and the exempt status for Federal income tax purposes (Check one)

☐ (1) HAS NOT CHANGED DURING PRECEDING 12 MONTHS   ☐ (2) HAS CHANGED DURING PRECEDING 12 MONTHS (If changed, publisher must submit explanation of change with this statement.)

| 10. | EXTENT AND NATURE OF CIRCULATION | AVERAGE NO. COPIES EACH ISSUE DURING PRECEDING 12 MONTHS | ACTUAL NO. COPIES OF SINGLE ISSUE PUBLISHED NEAREST TO FILING DATE |
|---|---|---|---|
| A. | TOTAL NO. COPIES (Net Press Run) | 1900 | 2010 |
| B. | PAID CIRCULATION | | |
| 1. | SALES THROUGH DEALERS AND CARRIERS, STREET VENDORS AND COUNTER SALES | 115 | 139 |
| 2. | MAIL SUBSCRIPTION | 916 | 906 |
| C. | TOTAL PAID CIRCULATION (Sum of 10B1 and 10B2) | 1031 | 1045 |
| D. | FREE DISTRIBUTION BY MAIL, CARRIER OR OTHER MEANS SAMPLES, COMPLIMENTARY, AND OTHER FREE COPIES | 89 | 188 |
| E. | TOTAL DISTRIBUTION (Sum of C and D) | 1120 | 1233 |
| F. | COPIES NOT DISTRIBUTED | | |
| 1. | OFFICE USE, LEFT OVER, UNACCOUNTED, SPOILED AFTER PRINTING | 780 | 777 |
| 2. | RETURN FROM NEWS AGENTS | | |
| G. | TOTAL (Sum of E, F1 and 2 - should equal net press run shown in A) | 1900 | 2010 |

11. I certify that the statements made by me above are correct and complete

SIGNATURE AND TITLE OF EDITOR, PUBLISHER, BUSINESS MANAGER, OR OWNER

*[signature]*   Vice-President

PS Form 3526, June 1985   (See instruction of reverse)   (Page 1)